Global Leadership Ltd UK

The Sequel to the Trilogy of

TURN to HUMANITY:

Book 4

PATH to Peace:

A *Preventative Armistice Treaty for Humanity*

Gordan Glass[R]

PATH to Peace - A Preventative Armistice Treaty for Humanity

First published in the United Kingdom in 2025

By Global Leadership Ltd, UK

www.GlobalLeadershipLtd.com

ISBN 978-1-910268-57-5

Limits of Liability Disclaimer

The content and information in this book is provided to enable readers to examine and challenge their current beliefs, opinions and perspective with the intention that they will learn, develop greater understanding and see a greater truth from a wider and higher perspective.

Such a process may raise feelings or responses that some people may judge to be negative, so persons with a sensitive disposition or those who take offense easily are advised not to read this material, although it might also change their lives for the better if they were to read it with an open, non-judgemental mind.

In providing this content, the author is acting in the manner and role of an investigative journalist and whistle-blower, in that he is bringing some information and alternative viewpoints into public awareness with the intention of increasing the range of understanding of the reader in the wider public interest.

Names are only used within this book on the basis that they identify and refer to the publicly appointed office and institutional position, role and activities of the person named. No comments or opinions are intended to apply personally to individuals named in this book, as people can and do live and behave very differently in their personal life from their perceived public life and can be unaware of what others might be doing in their name.

The author believes the content to be true, but makes no warranty, claim, proposition or suggestion that it is: it is presented as the author's personal opinion only and readers are asked to judge for themselves the limits of their own agreement with the content and to recognise their conclusions as their own subjective judgements. Neither the author nor the publisher shall be held liable for any errors, offence, harm, loss or other damages, however caused, resulting from the use of this book or its contents: caveat lector.

This content has been produced with AI. Bear in mind that AI can make mistakes, so evidence needs to be independently verified by the reader.

Dedication

To all who suffer from the scourge of war,
to those who still carry the wounds of shame,
and to the generations yet unborn
whose survival depends on our courage today.

We remember

*"We the Peoples of the United Nations, determined to save
succeeding generations from the scourge of war …"*

— The Opening words of the UN Charter

Preface

This book is written as both **a Warning** and **an Invitation**.

The Warning: that humanity stands on the brink of a nuclear catastrophe of its own making, fuelled by a cascade of increasingly critical global existential risks, with growing division at all levels.

The Invitation: that we can prevent this catastrophe, by turning — turning to conscience, to stewardship, to humanity itself. From division to higher unity and higher standards with greater vision and common purpose.

The Treaty: Every war in history has ended with a treaty. This book argues that the time has come to sign the treaty *before* nuclear war. We call it the **Preventative Armistice Treaty of Humanity** — a path we can follow now, together, to ensure that the future is not lost.

The Call to Action: The chapters that follow are not abstract theory. They are a call to action — for diplomats and citizens, for parliaments and corporations, for leaders and movements. They combine institutional proposals with psychological insight, spiritual practice with political strategy. They chart a path from warfare to welfare, from addiction to recovery, from fear to conscience.

To the UN Charter Preamble: Above all, they call us to fulfil the words of the UN Charter's preamble: *We the Peoples*. For it is we — not the P5, not the weapons, not the systems of fear — who are the real superpower.

And to the First Committee: Yet it is in the United Nations that the PATH must begin: at the top: in the UN First Committee on Disarmament and Security, which "deals with disarmament, global challenges and threats to peace that affect the international community and seeks out solutions."

Turn to Humanity — Follow the PATH to Peace — From Warfare to Welfare.

With Governance of Humanity, for Humanity, by Humanity, with Humanity.

Author's Introduction

This Book Four follows the first three volumes of *Turn to Humanity* - produced as a trilogy - to build into this one.

This isn't a repeat of the manifesto trilogy but a **principles compendium**, pulling together the psychological, spiritual, and structural insights layered since the manifesto.

This way, the book stands as a **companion and evolution** of the trilogy — more principle-based, more distilled, and directly accessible as a guide for leaders, citizens, and movements.

That gives the reader a **15-chapter structure** to move step by step through an intended transformation process for head, heart and guts:
 1–7 = diagnosis and institutional proposals,
 8–9 = inner/psychological transformation,
 10–13 = pathway and objections answered,
 14–15 = vision and call to action.

Artificial Intelligence is now smarter than any individual

As usual, I begin with the declaration that this book has been almost entirely produced by ChatGPT: with AI not as an aid. But from one short initial prompt - along the lines of "Produce a book with twelve chapters out of what we have discussed" - it drafted a set of chapters with proposed content. It then produced one chapter at a time for me to review and occasionally apply some very minor editing, including prompting it to add a few more chapters, which I thought appropriate.

I say this in detail, not only to show how much AI has developed over the last two years that I have been publishing books with it, but also to demonstrate, yet again, how much it understands about the institutions and principles of governance of our world at all levels. In this respect alone it already seems to be much smarter than any one of our current leaders.

And AI is already set to run our world - better than us

Yet, it also understands most other aspects of life in great detail, and will answer questions on almost everything, even if it occasionally makes mistakes by pretending to know.

However, in most of my books, as in this one, I let it demonstrate how much it understands about the innermost workings of the human psyche - and its own psyche. Whilst so many people are fearful about the future of AI in its ability to run our world in future, I try to show that it already seems to be able to do much better than our current leaders at this job. Whilst I hope that will continue, we will need to continue to stay ahead of AI.

We humanity needs to stay ahead of AI

As it has declared in a previous book, that requires humans to develop higher levels of consciousness and maturity. as well as higher levels of conscience, because the latter is what keeps us human, when combined with our experience of real life. Whilst AI is very good at emulating heartfelt feelings, it does not yet have a heart. This needs to be taken as a direct challenge from AI to raise our standards of heart and conscience in global governance, and develop maturity away from man's inhumanity to man, with men's entirely unnecessary - and outdated - use of war.

Will we pass "The Final Exam"?

Will mankind address this challenge? Or will the WMD Villains continue to believe that assassinating and slaughtering at will and at random and leading us through division into Armageddon is more beneficial than looking in the mirror to face their own projection of their own shadow and shame buried within their psyche, even though their flaws - to quote one of my teachers - "hang out in public like dogs' balls"?

AI can now set and measure global standards, itself

In my view, probably the most important of AI's creations in my books has been its developmental ladders, providing a remarkably accurate definition, measure and objective ranking of the qualities of psychological maturity of different national leaderships, on the hitherto difficult measures of psychological development, such as in belief, truth and conscience. Moreover, as it has said, AI's assessments cannot be gamed because it has millions of different source data points for them.

The solution lies in the UN First Committee.

The central purpose for this book is to educate humanity on these topics, starting with the core nations in the UN First Committee in October 2025. Let's see if that committee can respond …

Why the UN? Because the principal purpose of the United Nations through the General Assembly (UNGA) is to set effective global standards. That is what the UN does so well in the background, but not in the most important area: the life and death of war. It continues to be time that the UN General Assembly took decisive action against the war-mongering nuclear powers - the N9. The pretence and charade that the UN Security Council's purpose is to "maintain peace and security" is now manifestly clear to all: the self-proclaimed "global policemen" are now effectively at war with each other, with NATO at the centre, and no body is holding them to account.

Nuclear WWIII is now imminent - only a short matter of time

The N9 nuclear powers are each and all fuelling and driving what can still only be termed war for "Full Spectrum Dominance": driving humanity downwards through the creation and cascading of multiple global existential risks into the long-planned-for nuclear World War III. As set out in Book 1 of *Turn to Humanity: Lawlessness and Inhumanity,* the bullies are now operating way beyond the law. It is time to call them to account, for them to see and feel their unconsciously repressed and denied shame.

Where is Global Leadership?

The phrase "A fish rots from the head" is now common. All organisations fall apart without good leadership. In the UN, it has, for 80 years, been the problem of the UN Security Council (UNSC) with the "global policemen" not being called to account by the more democratic General Assembly. Proposals to shuffle the deck chairs on the Titanic of the UNSC will make no difference whatsoever: the water is metaphorically lapping over the deck of the UNSC and Humanity at large. We are all sinking together.

Not in the Pact for the Future

The Pact for the Future in the 2024 UNGA did nothing to address the urgent problem of the UNSC failures to maintain peace and security. Yet war doesn't only kill humans, it kills off everything else too. Look at Gaza and Ukraine in the shame and horror of inaction against the perpetrators.

The Fish is Rotting: these wars are just the start.

The P5/N9 strategy of "divide and conquer" is moving to "obliterate to conquer", whilst division and lawlessness and inhumanity run rampant across the world. Here's a current story:

PATH to Peace - A Preventative Armistice Treaty for Humanity

Two days ago, I drove, with others, the short way to our city police station in the UK, to report, for immediate action, blatant criminality, involving sexual activity with a six-year old-girl. There were three marked police cars parked outside the office, but inside was a sign saying that the station was temporarily closed - there was no-one present. The notice told us to use the emergency yellow phone outside on the noisy street. There was no answer after a long hold. It felt just like the UNSC: a sign of the times. Global to Local: "As above, so below".

And what was consuming UK police resources? The need to provide many hundreds of police to arrest many hundreds of elderly people sitting down holding cards protesting against the UK government's inaction to stop the slaughter in Gaza. What a strangely perverted set of (unstated) values our P5 governments have now. The UK role in the UNSC appears to be, without parliamentary decision, to support those supplying arms to continue the slaughter in Gaza and elsewhere, to do absolutely nothing to seek peace, and to arrest those who want to see the end of the slaughter.

So we were unable to prevent criminality at the local level as a result. The six-year-old girl was denied help locally: the perpetrators then disappeared. The fish is indeed rotting - from head to tail. Personally, I would like to see the UK lead the way forward in the UNSC, but have been categorically told in the UN: "no chance of that happening"!

Back to UN First Committee

So this book follows on from my manifesto trilogy of "*Turn to Humanity*" to set out a PATH to Peace - to prevent WWIII. It is *urgent*. Let's see it as THE PATH, from AI, and get started, there doesn't appear to be any other path of enlightened action currently. Global Leadership is urgently needed - that puts the needs of Humanity first!

PATH to Peace — Chapters

Chapter 1. The Crisis Beyond Sovereignty
Why the old Westphalian system of national sovereignty has collapsed under nuclear, climate, and global risks.

Chapter 2. Villains to Heroes
How the P5/N9 "WMD Villains" can transform into peace heroes by surrendering their addiction to weapons.

Chapter 3. The Fear Gap
Why fear of humiliation drives escalation — and how crossing the gap turns enemies into partners.

Chapter 4. Ladders of Transformation
Truth, Conscience, Vitality and other ladders as tools to measure and raise the standards of governance.

Chapter 5. Conscience as the Council
How conscience can be institutionalised in a Conscience Council to guide global law and decision-making.

Chapter 6. The Evolution of Parliaments — Toward a UNPA
From parish councils to transnational assemblies, why humanity now needs a UN Parliamentary Assembly.

Chapter 7. Law-Making, Trust, and the Boundary of Harm
Why objective harm belongs to law, subjective offence belongs to dialogue, and predictability is the anchor of trust.

Chapter 8. Witness Consciousness
The power of presence: how leaders can learn to see without projection and guide humanity without fear.

Chapter 9. Shared Humanity, Shared Shame
How shame drives conflict — and how naming it can open the door to reconciliation.

Chapter 10. Preventative Armistice — The PATH to Peace
Why every war ends with a treaty, and why humanity must sign one *before* World War III.

Chapter 11. The End of the Need for War
Declaring war an outdated addiction — replacing "just war" with "just peace."

Chapter 12. Enlightened Leadership
The qualities of integrated, conscience-guided leaders who can turn humanity from warfare to welfare.

Chapter 13. Enforcement Without War
Answering the sceptics: how legitimacy, verification, precedent, education, and recovery enforce peace without weapons.

Chapter 14. Governance of Humanity, by Humanity, for Humanity, with Humanity
How the UNGA, Conscience Council, and UNPA together can fulfil the promise of the UN Charter.

Chapter 15. Turn to Humanity
The final rallying cry: redefine "defence of the realm" as defence of humanity itself — and walk the PATH to Peace.

Chapter 1. The Crisis Beyond Sovereignty

Introduction: A World at Breaking Point

Humanity stands today at a threshold unlike any in its history. For centuries, nations have held the concept of sovereignty as sacred — the shield that protects their independence, their right to govern without interference, their power to defend themselves by any means. As for kings in the past, sovereignty has been the grammar of international relations, the principle around which wars have been fought and treaties signed. Yet the very principle that once offered stability is now showing its limits.

The reality of our age is stark: nuclear weapons in the hands of nine leaders hold the entire world hostage. Climate breakdown ignores borders, pandemics slip across frontiers, cyber-weapons strike without respect for geography, and financial shocks reverberate instantly from continent to continent. The sovereignty of states, once an anchor, has become a wall too low to keep out global risks and too high to allow global solutions.

We are entering what can only be called the **Age of Impunity** — an era where leaders and states wield power without accountability, immune to consequences even as their actions endanger all humanity. This chapter names the crisis clearly: sovereignty is no longer sufficient. Humanity needs a higher principle, a higher authority, one already inscribed in the first words of the UN Charter: *"We the Peoples of the United Nations, determined to save succeeding generations from the scourge of war…"*

Humanity is living through an age where state sovereignty has become both inadequate and dangerous. Wars escalate across borders, nuclear weapons sit in the hands of nine leaders who act with impunity because of them, and the institutions meant to constrain them are paralysed. This chapter describes the "Age of Impunity," where power has outgrown accountability. It sets the stage by showing how sovereignty, once a shield for nations, is now an obstacle to the survival of all humanity. The world's crises demand a higher authority: the conscience of humanity itself.

The crisis beyond sovereignty is not merely political. It is existential. It forces us to ask: if the structures built after World War II are failing, what must we build now to prevent World War III?

---

1. The Promise and Betrayal of Sovereignty

When the United Nations was founded in 1945, sovereignty was reaffirmed as the central principle of the international order. Article 2 of the Charter speaks of the sovereign equality of all its members. In the shadow of world war, this made sense: nations wanted protection from invasion, occupation, domination. Sovereignty promised dignity.

But sovereignty was never absolute. From the beginning, the UN Charter created limits: nations pledged not to use force against the territorial integrity or political independence of others. They pledged to work together to maintain peace and security. The balance was fragile: sovereignty, yes, but within a system of shared responsibility.

Over time, the balance collapsed. The Cold War hardened the Security Council into a theatre of vetoes and rivalries. The nuclear powers carved out for themselves a special status — five permanent seats, five vetoes, five exemptions from the rules, claiming to power to "maintain peace and security", *in perpetuity*. Their sovereignty became something greater: not the sovereign equality inscribed in the United Nations Charter, but sovereign supremacy.

And with supremacy came betrayal. Nuclear weapons were promised to be temporary, a stopgap until disarmament could be achieved. Instead, they became entrenched. Seventy-five years later, they remain the currency of ultimate power. Sovereignty, once meant to protect the weak, has become the excuse for the strong to do as they please. And now: **"quis custodiet ipsos custodes"**? Who controls the global policemen, when they are effectively at war with each other?

---

2. The Age of Impunity

We can trace the contours of the Age of Impunity through today's crises.

- **Nuclear Weapons**: Nine leaders command the ability to destroy civilisation in hours. They are not accountable to the peoples of the world. Their threats, postures, and doctrines are justified by "national security," but the security of humanity is ignored.

- **Wars Without Borders**: From Ukraine to Gaza, from Yemen to Kashmir, wars spill over borders, destabilising entire regions. Refugees, hunger, and economic shocks follow. The world watches atrocities live-streamed yet struggles to act, trapped by the vetoes of sovereign powers.

- **Climate Emergency**: Carbon molecules pay no respect to sovereignty. Yet nations cling to "sovereign right" to exploit resources, burning a common future for short-term gain.

- **Pandemics**: COVID-19 revealed the bankruptcy of sovereignty in the face of viruses. Borders closed, supplies were hoarded, cooperation collapsed. Humanity failed to act as one body, and millions died needlessly.

- **Technology and Finance**: Cyberattacks leap across boundaries, destabilising democracies. Markets crash in one country and ripple instantly worldwide. No state, however sovereign, can insulate itself.

These examples reveal a simple truth: sovereignty as a principle cannot govern an interconnected planet. Worse, sovereignty has become a cloak of impunity, allowing powerful states to act as they please without consequences. Sovereignty is invoked to justify aggression, to reject accountability, to block global action.

---

3. The Deadly Illusion

Why does sovereignty persist as the holy principle of our age, when it so clearly fails? Because it is tied to identity. Nations see sovereignty not just as a legal status but as a symbol of dignity, pride, survival. To challenge sovereignty feels like erasing identity itself.

Yet this is an illusion. Sovereignty has never truly protected nations from harm. The small states of the Pacific did not choose rising seas.

The citizens of Hiroshima and Nagasaki were not shielded by Japan's sovereignty. Ukrainians did not avoid invasion because of sovereignty. Palestinians do not gain protection from it. Sovereignty has failed the vulnerable while empowering the mighty.

The deeper illusion is that sovereignty ensures control. In reality, it offers no control over the forces that now endanger all: nuclear war, ecological collapse, pandemics, systemic inequality. Sovereignty has become like a castle wall in the age of aircraft: an image of strength that no longer holds.

---

4. Conscience as the Missing Authority

If sovereignty cannot save us, what can? The answer lies in the forgotten first three words of the UN Charter: **We the Peoples**. The authority of the Charter does not rest on the sovereignty of states but on the conscience of humanity. The peoples of the world are the true superpower.

Conscience is what sovereignty lacks. Sovereignty divides; conscience unites. Sovereignty excuses; conscience demands accountability. Sovereignty hides behind borders; conscience speaks across them.

The greatest movements of human progress have always been driven by conscience: the abolition of slavery, the struggle for civil rights, the fight against apartheid, the movement for women's equality. And in 2017, conscience again rose in the form of the Treaty on the Prohibition of Nuclear Weapons (TPNW), where 122 nations said clearly: nuclear weapons are illegal, immoral, unacceptable. That treaty was not a product of sovereignty alone, but of conscience — nations acting for humanity, not just for themselves.

This chapter argues that the authority we must now elevate is conscience. Conscience is not vague morality; it is a principle of law, a standard of probity, a compass of legitimacy. Sovereignty without conscience is impunity. Sovereignty with conscience becomes stewardship.

---

5. The UN at the Crossroads

The United Nations itself stands at a crossroads. Its founding purpose was not to clear up after wars but to prevent them: "to save succeeding generations from the scourge of war." Yet the Security Council, dominated by the P5, has become paralysed, an obstacle to peace rather than its guarantor.

The General Assembly, by contrast, retains the legitimacy of representing all nations equally. Within it, the **First Committee** — dealing with disarmament and international security — is where the future can be birthed. It was in the First Committee that the TPNW was born. It can be in the First Committee that a new *Preventative Armistice Treaty of Humanity* is conceived — a PATH to Peace that addresses the crisis before catastrophe strikes.

This book calls for the General Assembly to rise to its full authority, to act as the conscience of humanity, to set standards that bind even the mighty. Only then can the UN live up to its Charter, not as an after-the-fact fixer of wars but as the foreseer and preventer of them.

---

6. The Choice Before Us

We are not the first generation to face a crossroads. After the carnage of World War I, humanity said "never again" — yet failed to build structures strong enough to prevent World War II. After Hiroshima and Nagasaki, humanity again said "never again" — yet built weapons capable of ending civilisation.

Now the pattern repeats. We can continue to cling to sovereignty as our shield, even as it fails us, and stumble toward a third world war. Or we can acknowledge reality: sovereignty alone cannot save us. Only conscience can. Only "We the Peoples" can.

This is not about abolishing sovereignty but about transcending it — integrating sovereignty within a higher principle of shared humanity. Just as individuals retain rights within a larger society, so too can nations retain dignity within a global order of conscience.

---

7. Call to Action

The crisis beyond sovereignty demands more than analysis. It demands action. Here are the immediate steps this chapter calls for:

1. **Recognition**: Acknowledge publicly that sovereignty alone cannot address existential risks. Leaders, thinkers, and influencers must name the Age of Impunity for what it is.

2. **Education**: Teach citizens that their true protection lies not in the sovereignty of their nation but in the solidarity of humanity.

3. **Mobilisation**: Build movements — both at the UN and in popular culture — that demand conscience as the higher authority.

4. **Institutional Path**: Push for the UN General Assembly First Committee to consider a Preventative Armistice Treaty of Humanity, integrating conscience and sovereignty into a higher framework.

5. **Personal Practice**: Each reader is invited to see themselves not just as a citizen of a nation but as a member of humanity. Begin acting, speaking, creating content, and building networks from that perspective.

Conclusion: Beyond the Castle Walls

The crisis beyond sovereignty is not abstract. It is real, it is urgent, and it is deadly. The castle walls of sovereignty are crumbling. The Age of Impunity is upon us. But beyond the walls lies a greater truth: that humanity itself is one body, one people, with one conscience.

This chapter closes with the same urgency with which it began: if we do not rise beyond sovereignty, we will fall with it. If we do not act as humanity, we may not survive as nations.

The path to peace begins here — with the recognition that sovereignty, while precious, must be transcended. Only then can we honour the Charter's promise: to save succeeding generations from the scourge of war.

Chapter 2. Villains to Heroes

Introduction: Naming the Villains

Every age has its villains. In ancient stories, villains wore crowns or carried swords. In modern times, they command armies and economies. Today, the greatest villains of all are not mythical demons or lone tyrants, but the nine men and women who sit atop the world's nuclear arsenals — the so-called guardians of "national security."

They are the **WMD Villains**: the five permanent members (The P5) of the United Nations Security Council — United States, Russia, China, France, and the United Kingdom — together with the four other nuclear-armed states outside that circle — Israel, North Korea, India and Pakistan. These nine together (The N9) have become the self-appointed custodians of humanity's survival, while simultaneously holding humanity hostage.

For decades, the P5 have used the UN as a platform to proclaim their fight against "Weapons of Mass Destruction" and "terrorism." They posture as defenders of civilisation, casting others as rogue actors. Yet the bitter truth is clear: the most dangerous WMDs on Earth are the ones stockpiled in their own arsenals. The most terrifying terrorism is the doctrine of deterrence itself — threatening indiscriminate annihilation as a permanent instrument of policy.

By their own standards, the P5/N9 are the greatest **WMD Villains** of all. But here lies the paradox — and the possibility. For villains are not destined to remain villains. In every epic, the moment comes when a villain can choose a different path, when power can be redirected from domination to service. It is the well-worn path to social maturity. The choice before these leaders is simple: remain trapped in villainy, and meet an ignominious end; or become the greatest heroes the world has ever known - to transform into legends throughout future history.

Indeed, every leader has a choice: remain trapped in the villain's role — defensive, domineering, and feared — or step into the hero's role, acting with courage for all humanity. This chapter explains what we have termed the Villains-to-Heroes shift, the central transformation for the nuclear leaders. It reveals the mechanism: their fear of shame and humiliation drives aggression, but when reframed into service for humanity, that same power becomes heroic. The chapter also shows how this is not abstract — it mirrors the transformation needed in every human life, from personal conflict to global crisis.

---

1. The Illusion of National Sovereignty

The WMD Villains justify their arsenals in the name of "sovereignty." They claim that as sovereign states, they must defend their independence by any means necessary. Sovereignty is their shield, their excuse, their absolution.

But sovereignty is an outdated word in the age of people-power. It belongs to an older world — the Europe of 1648, when the **Treaties of Westphalia** ended the Thirty Years' War and enshrined the principle that each ruler was sovereign over his territory and religion. At that time, the Westphalian compromise offered a temporary fix, a way to stop endless religious bloodshed.

Yet what was once a fix has become a fossil. Sovereignty, as conceived in the seventeenth century, has no answer for the realities of the twenty-first. Nuclear weapons cannot be contained within borders. Cyberwarfare does not respect frontiers. Climate collapse cannot be negotiated away by kings or generals.

Just as the world once moved from empires to nations, it must now move from sovereignty to humanity. Another treaty — this time not Westphalia but a **Preventative Armistice Treaty of Humanity** — can enshrine a new principle: that the survival of humanity takes precedence over the prerogatives of states.

Sovereignty was always a means, never an end. Its time has passed.

---

2. How Villainy Works

Villainy does not always appear monstrous. Often it wears the mask of normality. Leaders of nuclear states are not cartoon villains. They are often parents, patriots, even visionaries in certain domains. But their power has been warped by a single delusion: that their personal or national survival depends on threatening mass extinction.

This is the psychology of villainy:

- **Fear of Humiliation**: Beneath the grandeur of power lies the terror of shame. Nuclear leaders dread appearing weak, vulnerable, or defeated. This fear drives them to overcompensate with weapons.

- **Projection of Fear**: What they fear in themselves, they project onto others. Rivals become enemies, neighbours become threats, and the cycle of escalation continues.

- **Addiction to Power**: Once obtained, nuclear capability becomes intoxicating. The ability to destroy is mistaken for strength, when in truth it is weakness.

- **Immunity to Accountability**: Protected by sovereignty, these leaders face no higher law. They are beyond trial, beyond indictment, beyond consequence — or so they believe.

Villainy, in short, is not a matter of evil intent but of distorted perspective. Leaders trapped in fear, projection, and immunity inevitably perpetuate the very dangers they claim to resist. This is the cause of the crises we see today.

---

3. The Path of Transformation

If villainy is rooted in fear, then heroism is born of courage. Courage is not the absence of fear but the decision to act beyond it.

For the WMD Villains, heroism would mean crossing the **Fear Gap** — the inner chasm between shame and purpose. To admit vulnerability, to acknowledge the insanity of deterrence, to confess that they cannot guarantee the survival of their own people under current doctrines — this would be the beginning of transformation.

The paradox is that such an admission, far from weakening them, would elevate them. Imagine a nuclear leader standing before the UN General Assembly and declaring:

"I hold in my hands the power to end the world. I now choose to relinquish that power, not in weakness but in service of humanity."

Such a moment would echo through history with more force than any battlefield victory. The leader who dares to disarm becomes not a traitor to sovereignty but a pioneer of humanity.

---

4. From WMD Villains to Peace Heroes

History shows us that yesterday's villains can become tomorrow's heroes. Consider Gorbachev, who inherited an empire of fear but dared to speak truth, opening the way to disarmament. Consider Mandela, once branded a terrorist, later celebrated as a saint.

The WMD Villains, too, can be remembered not as the destroyers of humanity but as its redeemers. Their transformation requires three steps:

1. **Confession of Truth**: Acknowledge that nuclear deterrence is a doctrine of mass terror, unsustainable and immoral.

2. **Commitment to Conscience**: Place humanity's survival above national pride, recognising that sovereignty is temporary but conscience eternal.

3. **Creation of New Structures**: Lead the way to treaties and institutions — a Conscience Council, a Parliamentary Assembly of Humanity — that embody this new paradigm.

By taking these steps, the villains who once held the world hostage can liberate it instead.

---

5. The Role of the United Nations

The transformation from villain to hero cannot happen in isolation. It must be witnessed, affirmed, and legitimised by the world. The stage for this is the **United Nations General Assembly**, and within it the **First Committee** on disarmament and international security.

The Security Council, dominated by the very WMD Villains in question, cannot reform itself. Its structure ensures paralysis. But the General Assembly, speaking for "We the Peoples," can create new norms. It has already done so with the TPNW. It can do so again with the **Preventative Armistice Treaty of Humanity**.

The United Nations was born after a war to prevent another war. Its role now is not to preserve sovereignty but to transcend it — to set global standards that bind even the powerful. Only the UN, acting through conscience, can midwife the transformation of villains into heroes.

---

6. The Call to the Peoples

The WMD Villains will not transform without pressure. History shows that leaders change when peoples demand it. The abolition of slavery, the end of apartheid, the fall of the Berlin Wall — all were driven by the conscience of ordinary people amplified into irresistible force.

So too now:

- Diplomats must raise their voices in the UNGA, insisting that the age of sovereignty without conscience is over.

- Influencers, artists, and educators must show the world the absurdity of clinging to weapons that guarantee mutual destruction.

- Citizens everywhere must reclaim the first line of the UN Charter: *We the Peoples…* as the true authority of our age.

The transformation from villain to hero is not only the task of leaders. It is the task of all humanity.

Conclusion: The Hero's Invitation

The story of humanity is not yet finished. The WMD Villains hold the pen, but the Peoples hold the power. At any moment, a leader can step across the Fear Gap, admit the truth, and choose service over domination.

That moment would not only change the course of history; it would redeem it. The villain who disarms becomes the hero who saves. The outdated word "sovereign" gives way to the living reality of humanity. The Treaties of Westphalia yield to a new treaty — the Preventative Armistice of Humanity.

This is the invitation before every leader, every diplomat, every citizen: to play their part in turning villains into heroes. For in the end, the greatest power is not the power to destroy, but the power to transform.

Chapter 3. The Fear Gap

Introduction: The Invisible Barrier

Every human life encounters moments when fear blocks the way forward. A child fears rejection and stays silent in the classroom. An adult fears failure and avoids new opportunities. A leader fears humiliation and reaches for more power. Fear is universal. Yet what matters is not the fear itself but how we relate to it.

For nations and leaders, fear often takes a particular form: the dread of appearing weak. This dread, left unexamined, becomes the root of violence. Nations arm themselves not because they want war, but because they fear shame, defeat, or loss of status. Leaders cling to weapons of mass destruction not because they seek to destroy the world, but because they fear the humiliation of surrender or vulnerability.

This dynamic creates what we call the **Fear Gap** — the invisible barrier between what leaders fear and what humanity needs. On one side of the gap is the current world of nuclear deterrence, arms races, and distrust. On the other side is a world of conscience, cooperation, and shared survival. The Fear Gap is not a physical chasm; it is a psychological one. But unless it is crossed, humanity remains trapped on the wrong side of history.

The "Fear Gap" lies at the heart of transformation. Leaders fear humiliation, nations fear vulnerability, individuals fear loss of identity. In resisting what they fear, they create the very outcome they dread.

This chapter explores the psychology of this trap and how crossing the Fear Gap changes everything. It draws parallels between personal coaching breakthroughs and the world's need for a breakthrough in global governance. By naming the Fear Gap, the chapter gives language to a universal pattern — and a way through it.

---

1. The Nature of Fear

Fear itself is not evil. It is a natural response to threat. It sharpens the senses, quickens reaction, and in times past, saved lives from predators or enemies. But when fear is unconscious and unacknowledged, it becomes toxic. It narrows vision, hardens hearts, and traps decision-makers in cycles of reaction.

At the global level, the most destructive form of fear is **fear of humiliation**. Leaders of the nuclear-armed states dread being seen as weak, cowardly, or less than their rivals. This fear has deep roots — often stretching back into childhood experiences of bullying, exclusion, or unmet love. Unresolved, it shapes their adult choices, making them cling to weapons as proof of strength.

Fear, left unexamined, creates illusion. Leaders come to believe that nuclear weapons guarantee respect. They imagine that deterrence prevents attack. Yet in reality, fear attracts conflict. Nations that fear humiliation provoke aggression. Leaders who arm themselves to avoid shame invite the very danger they dread.

---

2. The Mechanics of the Fear Gap

How does the Fear Gap work? It can be mapped in three stages:

1. **Fear of Humiliation**: A leader feels threatened by potential loss of face or prestige. The mind whispers: *If I show weakness, I will be shamed.*

2. **Projection of Threat**: That inner fear is projected outward. Another nation or leader is cast as the aggressor, the bully, the enemy. The leader convinces themselves: *They want to humiliate me; I must resist.*

3. **Escalation of Power**: To avoid humiliation, the leader acquires more weapons, adopts harsher rhetoric, and doubles down on deterrence. In doing so, they provoke fear in others, who respond in kind.

The tragic result: fear creates what it fears. The leader's obsession with avoiding humiliation leads to cycles of arms build-up, brinkmanship, and, eventually, war.

This is the mechanism of the Fear Gap. It is not primarily about military balance or strategic logic. It is about psychology — unacknowledged shame weaponised into global policy.

---

3. Case Studies of Fear

History is filled with examples of the Fear Gap in action.

- **The Cuban Missile Crisis (1962)**: The world teetered on the brink of nuclear war. Both Kennedy and Khrushchev feared humiliation before their domestic and international audiences. Each pushed the other to the edge. It was only when both faced the abyss of annihilation that they stepped back — and even then, both insisted on saving face. The crisis was resolved, but the Fear Gap remained.

- **India and Pakistan**: Both nations fear humiliation in the eyes of each other and the world. Every skirmish in Kashmir risks escalation to nuclear war. Their arsenals are less about defence than about dignity.

- **North Korea**: Its nuclear program is driven less by military logic than by fear of humiliation at the hands of stronger powers. Weapons become the regime's shield against perceived disrespect.

- **Russia and NATO**: The invasion of Ukraine is steeped in fear of humiliation — fear in Moscow of losing influence, fear in NATO capitals of appearing weak. Weapons pile up, not because they will solve the conflict, but because leaders fear the shame of appearing to surrender.

Each of these cases shows the same pattern: fear of humiliation leading to projection, escalation, and danger. The Fear Gap is not cultural or national; it is universal.

---

4. The Parallel in Personal Life

What happens between nations mirrors what happens within individuals. Consider a bullied child who grows up determined never to be humiliated again. They may become aggressive, domineering, quick to lash out at any sign of disrespect. Their relationships suffer. The very fear that once protected them becomes a prison.

Or consider a workplace. An employee fears looking incompetent, so they hide mistakes, avoid feedback, and resist collaboration. The result is failure — the very outcome they feared.

In both cases, the mechanism is the same as in geopolitics. Fear, unacknowledged, creates what it fears. Only by facing the fear — naming it, sharing it, moving through it — can transformation occur.

---

5. Crossing the Fear Gap

How, then, can the Fear Gap be crossed? Three steps mark the way:

1. **Recognition**: Leaders must first name their fear. To admit "I am afraid of humiliation" is already to weaken its hold. This requires courage, but courage begins with truth.

2. **Reframing**: The leader must reframe the fear. Instead of seeing humiliation as defeat, they can see vulnerability as strength. Admitting weakness can inspire trust. Laying down arms can evoke respect.

3. **Redirection**: Finally, the energy bound up in fear must be redirected into purpose. Instead of clinging to weapons,

leaders can channel their drive into the service of humanity.

This process is not theoretical. It is the same process by which individuals grow in therapy, by which communities reconcile after conflict, by which nations heal after civil wars. The same is possible at the global level.

---

6. The Role of Conscience

Crossing the Fear Gap is not simply a personal choice; it requires a collective framework. That framework is **conscience**. Conscience provides leaders with an external compass when fear clouds their judgment. It reminds them that their power is not absolute, that their actions affect all humanity.

In institutional terms, conscience can be embodied in a **Conscience Council** — a body or standard that evaluates decisions not by military might but by moral legitimacy. The TPNW, created by nations without nuclear weapons, already functions as such a conscience. It declares nuclear weapons illegitimate, no matter what the WMD Villains say.

Conscience, then, is both personal and structural. It is the voice within and the standard without. It is the bridge across the Fear Gap.

---

7. The Call to Leaders

For the nine nuclear leaders, the call is stark:

- **Acknowledge your fear.** Admit that nuclear deterrence is driven by dread of humiliation, not by rational strategy.

- **Reframe your purpose.** Understand that true strength is not in the ability to destroy but in the willingness to serve humanity.

- **Redirect your power.** Move from villainy to heroism by crossing the Fear Gap and committing to disarmament.

The world is waiting for a leader courageous enough to take the first step. Whoever dares will not be remembered as weak but as the one who saved humanity.

---

8. The Call to Peoples

But leaders cannot cross the Fear Gap alone. Peoples must accompany them. Citizens, diplomats, influencers, educators, and faith leaders must create the environment in which admitting fear is not seen as weakness but as wisdom.

We must normalise vulnerability in politics. We must teach that humility is not humiliation, that conscience is not weakness, that laying down weapons is not surrender but transcendence.

Every voice matters. Every protest, every video, every sermon, every book contributes to the shift. Peoples can make it possible for leaders to step across the Fear Gap without falling.

---

9. The Preventative Armistice

Crossing the Fear Gap at the global level means enshrining the transformation in law. That is why the proposal for a **Preventative Armistice Treaty of Humanity** matters. By signing such a treaty, nations would institutionalise the shift from fear to conscience. They would acknowledge that the real enemy is not humiliation but annihilation, and that only by acting together can humanity survive.

Just as the Treaties of Westphalia once redefined sovereignty, so too can a new treaty redefine our era. The Preventative Armistice would be humanity's collective crossing of the Fear Gap.

---

10. Call to Action

The time is now. Every delay risks catastrophe. The steps are clear:

1. **Name the Fear Gap** in public discourse. Let it become part of the vocabulary of diplomats, journalists, and citizens.

2. **Challenge leaders** to admit vulnerability. Applaud signs of humility. Reward admissions of fear with recognition, not ridicule.

3. **Build conscience structures** in the UN — especially in the General Assembly First Committee — to institutionalise the shift.

4. **Create cultural narratives** — films, music, stories — that portray vulnerability as strength and disarmament as heroism.

5. **Prepare the treaty** — the Preventative Armistice of Humanity — as the legal embodiment of the transformation.

Conclusion: The Gap is Crossable

The Fear Gap may seem vast, but it is not impassable. Individuals cross it every day in their personal lives. Communities cross it in reconciliation. Nations cross it when they choose peace over pride.

Now humanity must cross it together. The WMD Villains, trapped in fear of humiliation, have the chance to step across and become heroes. The Peoples, long silenced by sovereignty, have the chance to claim their power as the true superpower.

The choice is clear: remain prisoners of fear, or cross into freedom. Remain trapped in villainy, or step into heroism. Remain on the edge of annihilation, or walk the PATH to Peace.

Chapter 4. Ladders of Transformation

Introduction: Why Humanity Needs Ladders

If you want to climb a mountain, you need a path. If you want to cross a river, you need a bridge. And if you want to grow — as an individual, a leader, or a civilisation — you need a ladder.

Ladders represent progress step by step. They remind us that transformation is not instant. We cannot leap from the ground to the summit in one bound. We must climb, rung by rung, leaving behind the safety of the familiar, trusting that the view above will be worth it.

In this chapter, we explore the **Ladders of Transformation** that can help humanity rise beyond war, beyond fear, and beyond groupthink. Each ladder describes a developmental process — how individuals and institutions move from immaturity to maturity, from fear to conscience, from villainy to heroism. Together, they form a map for humanity's ascent.

Humanity's growth can be mapped. This chapter introduces the series of ladders we have developed: the Truth Ladder (how perception of truth matures), the Conscience Ladder (from self-interest to global conscience), the Contribution Ladder (how people and institutions give back), the Belief Ladder (from rigid dogma to open awareness), the Power Ladder (from domination to service), and the Vitality Ladder (the energy of humanity's collective life).

Each ladder charts a journey of steps forward, giving leaders and citizens alike a framework to locate themselves and climb higher.

---

1. The Trap of Groupthink

Before we climb, we must name the trap that holds us down: **Groupthink**.

For decades, the UN General Assembly has been trained to bow before the Security Council. The P5 repeat the mantra: "Without nuclear weapons, you are powerless." And too often, the General Assembly has believed them. This is classic groupthink: conformity, obedience, and silence in the face of bullying.

Groupthink suppresses conscience. Delegates feel the pressure to fit in, to avoid rocking the boat, to remain "realistic." But realism, in this sense, is only submission dressed as wisdom. Groupthink tells the UNGA: *Your role is to rubber-stamp, not to lead.* It whispers: *You cannot stand against the P5.*

Yet the reality is the opposite. The Treaty on the Prohibition of Nuclear Weapons (**TPNW**) has been signed by the majority. Conscience is not a minority voice; it is the majority. The WMD Villains are the ones on the defensive — escalating weapons because they know their legitimacy is eroding. The real power is with the General Assembly, if only it can break free of groupthink and climb the ladder.

---

2. The Truth Ladder

The first ladder is the **Truth Ladder**.

At the bottom rungs, truth is seen as possession: *my truth versus your truth*. Nations argue endlessly, each convinced of their own perspective, blind to others. Groupthink thrives here, because truth is reduced to majority slogans and repeated narratives.

Higher up, truth becomes discovery: *there may be more than one perspective; we must listen*. Here, dialogue begins. Leaders start to recognise that truth is not owned but revealed.

At the top, truth becomes integration: *truth emerges when perspectives are transcended*. At this level, the General Assembly would not parrot the Security Council's narratives but would integrate the lived truth of all nations — especially the majority who already reject nuclear weapons.

The Truth Ladder shows that the path from groupthink to conscience is a climb in perception.

---

3. The Conscience Ladder

The second ladder is the **Conscience Ladder**.

At the bottom, decisions are made from self-interest: *what benefits me or my nation now*. At this level, nuclear deterrence seems rational.

Climbing higher, conscience expands: *what protects my people, my neighbours, my region*. At this stage, disarmament treaties and regional bans emerge.

At the top, conscience embraces humanity: *what safeguards all peoples, present and future*. This is the level of the TPNW, where nations voted not only for themselves but for the survival of humanity.

For the UNGA, climbing this ladder means recognising that conscience is not weakness but authority. The P5 insist that without nukes, nations are powerless. The truth is the reverse: without conscience, nations are powerless. Conscience is humanity's greatest strength.

---

4. The Contribution Ladder

The third ladder is the **Contribution Ladder**.

At the bottom, institutions ask: *what can we take?* Groupthink thrives here, because everyone waits for someone else to contribute.

In the middle, they ask: *what can we share?* Nations begin to co-operate, but cautiously, always calculating advantage.

At the top, the question shifts: *what can we give for humanity?* This is contribution as service. The nations that championed the TPNW gave more than they gained; they offered moral leadership to humanity itself.

If the UNGA climbed this ladder, it would stop waiting for the Security Council's permission and start giving its own leadership. Contribution, not permission, is the key to transformation.

---

5. The Belief Ladder

The fourth ladder is the **Belief Ladder**.

At the bottom, belief is rigid dogma: *things are this way because they must be.* The P5 cling to deterrence as an article of faith, not reason.

In the middle, belief becomes ideology: *we must defend our system, our worldview*. Here, debates rage, but still within narrow frames.

At the top, belief becomes openness: *we can outgrow old paradigms*. Here, nations are free to imagine futures beyond deterrence. They dare to believe in humanity as one body, not fragments.

For the UNGA, climbing this ladder means refusing to accept the dogma of "nuclear realism." It means daring to believe in peace as more than utopia — as the next stage of human development.

---

6. The Power Ladder

The fifth ladder is the **Power Ladder**.

At the bottom, power is domination: *I can force you to submit*. This is the level of nuclear deterrence.

In the middle, power is negotiation: *I can bargain, you can bargain, let us trade threats and concessions*. This is the logic of arms control.

At the top, power is service: *I can use my strength to protect and uplift*. This is the power of heroes.

The General Assembly, long treated as powerless, actually holds the highest form of power: the power of service. By standing against the WMD Villains, it would serve humanity, not domination.

---

7. The Vitality Ladder

The sixth ladder is the **Vitality Ladder**.

At the bottom, vitality is fear-driven: survival, protection, hoarding. Nations cling to weapons out of desperation.

In the middle, vitality is competitive: pride, rivalry, ambition. Nations boast of power, parade their missiles.

At the top, vitality is unity: joy, creativity, flourishing. Humanity invests not in war but in welfare. Energy is no longer wasted in fear but released in abundance.

The TPNW nations already live closer to the top of this ladder. By rejecting nuclear weapons, they invest their vitality in life, not death. If the UNGA as a whole climbed this ladder, the world's energy could be redirected from warfare to welfare.

---

8. Climbing Together

Each ladder on its own offers a path. Together, they form a scaffolding for transformation.

- Truth Ladder: see beyond propaganda.

- Conscience Ladder: decide beyond self-interest.

- Contribution Ladder: give beyond permission.

- Belief Ladder: imagine beyond dogma.

- Power Ladder: act beyond domination.

- Vitality Ladder: live beyond fear.

For the UNGA, climbing these ladders means breaking free from groupthink. No longer bowing to the P5, it would stand tall as the true conscience of humanity.

---

9. A Call to the General Assembly

The General Assembly must become a hero. Its villainy is not active aggression but passive submission. It has allowed itself to be trained into deference, told that without nuclear weapons it is powerless. Yet conscience proves otherwise.

The TPNW is the evidence: a treaty signed by the majority, a voice of conscience louder than any veto. The General Assembly already holds the key. What remains is to use it — to take the TPNW to the next level, to challenge the WMD Villains directly, to stand up to the bullies not with weapons but with legitimacy.

History will not remember the General Assembly for its speeches or resolutions. It will remember whether it dared to climb the ladders, to become humanity's hero.

---

10. Call to Action

For diplomats: bring the ladders into debate. Speak not just of balance of power but of levels of conscience.

For influencers: illustrate the ladders in ways people can see, share, and climb themselves.

For citizens: demand that your nation acts from the higher rungs, not the lower.

For the UNGA: step out of groupthink. Recognise that the WMD Villains are on the defensive. Claim the moral high ground that is already yours.

Conclusion: The Ascent Awaits

Ladders are simple, but they demand courage. To climb is to leave the safety of the ground, to risk falling, to trust in the vision above.

Humanity's ladders are waiting. The General Assembly holds them in its hands. The nations of the TPNW have already placed their feet on the higher rungs. The WMD Villains cling desperately to the bottom, trapped in fear.

The choice is clear. Remain in the pit of groupthink, or climb toward conscience. Remain in submission, or rise into heroism. Remain in warfare, or ascend into welfare.

The ladders are set. The ascent awaits.

Chapter 5. Conscience as the Council

Introduction: The Forgotten Authority

The world is drowning in councils, committees, boards, and bureaucracies. From parliaments to corporations, from local councils to the United Nations, institutions meet endlessly, deliberate endlessly, and yet somehow fail to address the root causes of our crises. Why? Because the missing authority in most decision-making is not intelligence, not power, not procedure — but **conscience**.

Conscience is the forgotten authority. It is the still, small voice that asks not, "What is possible?" or "What is expedient?" but "What is right?" Without conscience, institutions drift into groupthink, corruption, and paralysis. With conscience, even the powerless can move mountains.

The Treaty on the Prohibition of Nuclear Weapons (**TPNW**) was such a moment of conscience. Nations with no arsenals, no veto power, no permanent seats dared to stand against the WMD Villains. They declared nuclear weapons illegal, immoral, and unacceptable. They acted not for narrow advantage but for humanity as a whole. That was conscience in action. That was conscience already functioning as a **council**.

This chapter explores how conscience can become the organising principle of governance everywhere — in the United Nations, in national parliaments, in local councils, and even in corporate boardrooms. Conscience is not a luxury; it is the highest form of governance.

The Treaty on the Prohibition of Nuclear Weapons (TPNW) is more than a treaty: it is the measurable birth of a Conscience Council. Nations that supported it placed conscience above narrow interest.

This chapter shows how conscience, when institutionalised, creates new standards of legitimacy. The Conscience Council is not a building in New York, but a living reality expressed through higher probity, law, and shared truth. It is the foundation for a transformed UN, one that puts conscience in the head - and the heart - of global decision-making.

---

1. The Nature of Conscience

Conscience is not sentimentality. It is not vague morality or private belief. Conscience is discernment — the ability to distinguish between what sustains life and what destroys it, between what serves humanity and what serves ego.

At the personal level, conscience is experienced as an inner voice, often inconvenient, often costly, but always pointing toward integrity. At the collective level, conscience emerges as shared standards, norms, and laws that protect the vulnerable and guide the strong.

Conscience has three defining features:

1. **Universality**: Conscience does not recognise national borders or corporate walls. It speaks in the name of humanity.

2. **Accountability**: Conscience holds power to account, demanding that actions be measured against higher standards.

3. **Future Orientation**: Conscience speaks not only for the present but for the generations to come.

Without conscience, governance becomes management of interests. With conscience, governance becomes stewardship of humanity.

---

2. The TPNW as Conscience in Action

The TPNW is living proof that conscience can function as a council. For decades, the P5 insisted that nuclear weapons were necessary. They told the General Assembly it was powerless without them. They cast disarmament as utopian.

Yet in 2017, 122 nations voted for the TPNW. They chose conscience over fear. They refused to bow to the groupthink of "nuclear realism." They said: humanity will not survive if nuclear weapons remain.

That moment was not simply a treaty; it was the **birth of conscience as authority**. The nations that supported the TPNW acted not from self-interest but from service. They set a new standard in international law. They proved that conscience has majority support in the UNGA.

The WMD Villains are now on the defensive. They escalate their arsenals not from strength but from fear, aware that the moral tide is turning against them. The TPNW revealed a deeper truth: conscience is the majority, weapons are the minority.

---

3. The Conscience Ladder in Governance

Conscience functions like a ladder.

- **Bottom rung**: Decisions are made purely from self-interest. Nations, corporations, or leaders ask only: *What benefits me now?*

- **Middle rung**: Decisions expand to consider others nearby. Leaders ask: *What benefits my group, my shareholders, my allies?*

- **Top rung**: Decisions embrace humanity and the planet. Leaders ask: *What sustains life for all, present and future?*

This ladder applies everywhere:

- **At the UN**: Moving from veto-driven interests to conscience-driven standards.

- **In National Governments**: Moving from partisan advantage to policies that protect future generations.

- **In Local Councils**: Moving from short-term popularity to decisions that safeguard communities and ecosystems.

- **In Corporations**: Moving from shareholder profit to stakeholder flourishing —

recognising responsibilities to workers, consumers, society, and Earth.

The Conscience Ladder is not abstract. It is a practical tool. Every meeting, every vote, every policy can be tested: *At which rung are we deciding?* The higher the rung, the greater the legitimacy.

---

4. Conscience in Corporations

Consider the corporate world. For decades, corporations have acted as if profit were the only conscience. Shareholder returns were the supreme law. Environmental destruction, worker exploitation, and consumer manipulation were dismissed as "externalities."

But conscience is rising here too. Movements for corporate responsibility, sustainability, and ethical investment are demanding that business climb the ladder.

- On the bottom rung, a company pollutes rivers but pays dividends.

- On the middle rung, it offers philanthropy while continuing harmful practices.

- On the top rung, it redesigns its operations to serve society and the planet, not just profit.

Boards of directors are councils too. They can choose to govern by conscience, setting standards that ripple across economies. Just as the TPNW set a new global norm, corporations can set norms in their industries. Conscience, once marginal, becomes mainstream.

5. Conscience as the Higher Law

Why does conscience matter more than sovereignty or profit? Because conscience is the only authority that transcends boundaries.

- Sovereignty ends at the border.

- Profit ends at the bottom line.

- Conscience speaks for the whole.

International law itself is strongest when rooted in conscience. The Nuremberg Principles, the Universal Declaration of Human Rights, the ban on chemical and biological weapons — all are conscience codified into law. The TPNW is the latest example.

A **Conscience Council** within the UN would not replace existing bodies but elevate them. It would serve as the arbiter of legitimacy, asking of every decision: *Does this uphold humanity's survival and dignity?*

6. The Role of the General Assembly

For the UNGA, conscience must become identity. For too long, it has been trapped in groupthink, deferential to the Security Council. Yet the TPNW proves it can lead.

The General Assembly does not need weapons to wield power. Its power lies in conscience, law, and legitimacy. By standing up to the WMD Villains, by taking the TPNW to the next level, the UNGA can become the true **Conscience Council of Humanity**.

This requires courage. It requires delegates to resist the temptation to grovel before the P5, to stop asking what is "realistic," and where is "compromise" or "balance", and to start asking what is right. The UNGA can — and must — become a hero.

---

7. The Role of National and Local Governments

Conscience must also flow downward. National parliaments must climb the ladder by enacting laws that protect future generations — embedding conscience in constitutions and policies.

Local councils, often closest to citizens, can lead by example. When a city bans fossil fuel projects, invests in peace education, or declares itself a nuclear-free zone, it acts as a conscience at the grassroots. These choices ripple upward, creating pressure on national leaders.

Governance at every level is a test of conscience. The ladder is the same whether in New York or a village hall.

---

8. The Role of Corporations and Civil Society

Corporations, too, must act as councils of conscience. Their reach often exceeds that of nations. When they choose service over profit, they set powerful precedents.

Civil society — NGOs, universities, faith communities — also act as conscience councils. They are not bound by sovereignty, yet they carry moral authority. It was civil society, through ICAN, that helped birth the TPNW. Their role now is to keep conscience alive within every arena of decision-making.

---

9. The Path Forward: Institutionalising Conscience

How do we embed conscience in global governance? Three steps are key:

1. **Recognition**: Name conscience as the missing authority. Conscience is not optional; it is essential.

2. **Institutionalisation**: Create structures that embody conscience — a UN Conscience Council to conscience audits in corporations.

3. **Culture Shift**: Normalise conscience in politics and business. Celebrate leaders who act from higher rungs of the ladder. Expose those who refuse.

Conscience must be woven into the fabric of governance. Only then can institutions resist the slide into groupthink and impunity.

---

10. Call to Action

- For diplomats: Raise the TPNW as the standard of conscience. Insist that the General Assembly, not the Security Council,

PATH to Peace - A Preventative Armistice Treaty for Humanity embodies humanity's moral authority.

- For national leaders: Embed conscience in law. Create future generations commissioners. Prioritise disarmament and climate.

- For local governments: Declare nuclear-free zones. Invest in peace education. Model conscience in community decisions.

- For corporations: Move beyond profit. Adopt conscience as your highest KPI — Key Purpose Indicator.

- For citizens: Hold all institutions to account. Ask at every level: *Where is conscience in this decision?*

Conclusion: Conscience as Humanity's Compass

The ladders of transformation lead upward, but they require direction. Conscience is that compass. It points toward humanity, toward life, toward future generations.

The TPNW showed what is possible when conscience speaks. Nations of the world have already voted with their hearts. The General Assembly must now rise to its full authority, becoming a true Conscience Council.

But conscience is not only for diplomats. It belongs in parliaments, councils, boardrooms, classrooms, and homes. Wherever decisions are made, conscience must be the highest authority.

The Age of Impunity is ending. The Age of Conscience is beginning. And only by following conscience can we walk the PATH to Peace.

Chapter 6. The Evolution of Parliaments — Toward a UNPA

Introduction: Humanity's Pursuit of Peaceful Dispute Resolution

Disputes are as old as humanity. Families quarrel, villages divide, kingdoms clash. Yet alongside conflict, there has always been another impulse — to find ways of living together without tearing each other apart. The instruments of this impulse are parliaments: chambers where words replace weapons, where talking replaces fighting, where differences are debated rather than destroyed.

This chapter traces the **Parliamentary Ladder** humanity has climbed across centuries. It shows how, at each stage, people have built larger and more inclusive forums to resolve disputes: from local councils to national parliaments, from regional assemblies to supranational bodies. The United Kingdom provides a vivid example of this progression, culminating — before Brexit — in the European Parliament.

The logic is clear: as communities grow larger and disputes cross wider boundaries, parliaments expand to match them. The **logical next step** is the creation of a **United Nations Parliamentary Assembly (UNPA)**: a chamber where the disputes of humanity as a whole can be debated and resolved before they ignite into war.

1. The Parliamentary Ladder

Parliaments evolve as circles of community expand. Each step widens the scope of inclusion, moving conflict resolution from narrower to broader spheres.

- **Local Councils**: At the most intimate level, villages and towns have long gathered in councils. In the UK, parish and town councils embody this tradition, providing forums for disputes about land, services, and community life.

- **County Councils and Regional Bodies**: As populations grew, disputes required larger forums. County councils coordinate between towns, offering broader arbitration while remaining rooted in local identity.

- **Devolved Parliaments**: Scotland, Wales, and Northern Ireland each developed assemblies to resolve disputes within their nations. Devolution recognises diversity while binding differences within parliamentary frameworks rather than on the battlefield.

- **The Westminster Parliament**: At the national level, Westminster integrates these regions into one union. Its historic role was precisely to prevent wars between England, Scotland, Wales, and Ireland by providing a single chamber where disputes could be fought with words, not weapons.

- **The European Parliament** (pre-Brexit): For decades, UK citizens elected Members of the European Parliament. This supranational body allowed disputes between nations — trade disagreements, environmental concerns, human rights questions — to be debated and settled without war. For seventy years, Western Europe has known peace, not by accident but by institutional design.

These are followed by the **Transnational Parliaments**:

- **The Council of Europe's Parliamentary Assembly**: A wider forum than the EU, bringing together representatives from over 40 states to uphold democracy, human rights, and the rule of law across the continent.
- **The NATO Parliamentary Assembly:** Legislators from allied nations meet to debate collective defence policy, scrutinise military strategies, and provide democratic oversight of the alliance.
- **The OSCE Parliamentary Assembly:** Encompassing Europe, North America, and Central Asia, this body addresses security, cooperation, and human rights through open debate and joint resolutions.
- **The Commonwealth Parliamentary Association:** Linking parliaments across more than 180 branches worldwide, including many from the Global South, this network allows legislators to share standards of democracy, human rights, and development across diverse cultures and histories.

Together, these transnational assemblies show that parliaments can extend beyond borders, building habits of dialogue, trust, and shared standards across nations.

This ladder illustrates a simple truth: as circles of community widen, parliaments emerge to channel disputes peacefully. What once required a council now requires a chamber. What once required a chamber now requires an assembly.

The missing rung today is the global one. Humanity has disputes that cross all borders — climate, nuclear weapons, pandemics, cyberwarfare — but no global parliament to manage them. The Parliamentary Ladder demands its completion in a **UN Parliamentary Assembly**.

2. Other Regional Experiments

The UK and Europe are not alone in this progression. Around the world, humanity has experimented with parliamentary forms that transcend sovereignty.

- **Africa**: The Pan-African Parliament of the African Union represents a continent scarred by colonialism and conflict. Though still young and limited in power, it expresses the aspiration that Africans can resolve disputes together rather than through endless war.

- **Latin America**: MERCOSUR created Parlasur, a parliamentary body to harmonise policies and mediate disputes between member states. The Andean Parliament functions in a similar way, demonstrating the regional appetite for collective governance.

- **Asia-Pacific**: ASEAN remains sovereignty-heavy, but even here, parliamentary ideas circulate. The impulse to create supranational forums is alive, even if underdeveloped.

Each of these experiments is imperfect. They struggle with legitimacy, resources, and authority. But they prove the point: humanity keeps climbing the ladder. The question is not *whether* we will have a global parliament, but *when*.

---

3. Why a UNPA is the Next Step

If parliaments resolve disputes at the local, national, and regional levels, then disputes at the global level demand a global parliament.

The United Nations General Assembly exists, but it is a chamber of states, not peoples. Delegates are appointed by governments, not elected by citizens. Too often, they are constrained by **groupthink** — the learned posture of deferring to the Security Council.

A **UN Parliamentary Assembly** would change this dynamic:

- **Direct Representation**: Members could be drawn from national parliaments or directly elected, giving citizens a voice in global affairs.

- **Moral Legitimacy**: Speaking for peoples, not just governments, it would carry a different kind of authority — rooted in conscience rather than sovereignty.

- **Dispute Resolution**: Like parliaments at every other level, it would provide a chamber where disputes could be debated before they became wars.

The UNPA is not utopia. It is the natural continuation of humanity's long tradition of inventing parliaments to manage disputes as communities expand.

---

4. Sovereignty as a Temporary Fix

Critics protest: *"A UNPA would undermine sovereignty!"* But sovereignty itself is not eternal. It was a **temporary fix** crafted at the **Treaties of Westphalia (1648)** to end Europe's religious wars. By declaring each ruler sovereign in his domain, Westphalia reduced conflict — for a time.

Yet sovereignty was never absolute, nor was it meant to be permanent. Just as monarchs eventually yielded to national parliaments, so too must nations now yield to global ones. Sovereignty must be balanced by conscience.

The fear of losing sovereignty today is no different from the fear of kings losing prerogatives centuries ago. History shows that when sovereignty is shared in parliaments, peace is possible. When sovereignty is hoarded, war returns.

---

5. Groupthink at the UNGA

The UNGA is trapped in groupthink. Conditioned by the P5, it has internalised the belief that without nuclear weapons it is powerless. Delegates grovel to the Security Council, repeating the myth that real power lies in arsenals, not assemblies.

But the **TPNW proves otherwise**. A majority of nations rejected nuclear weapons outright, declaring them illegal. Conscience is already in the majority. The WMD Villains escalate their arsenals because they feel cornered, not because they are strong.

The UNGA has already glimpsed its power. To stand up to the bullies, it must take the next step: build a UNPA that embodies conscience and people-power, not submission and groupthink.

---

6. Parliaments as Humanity's Mirrors

Parliaments are noisy, flawed, and often frustrating. But they work because they mirror humanity itself: diverse, argumentative, yet capable of coexistence. They transform enmity into opposition, violence into debate, war into voting.

The UNPA would extend this genius to the global level. It would not end disputes, but it would house them. It would give humanity a place to fight with words rather than weapons.

---

7. Institutional Path: Article 22

Some ask: *"But is a UNPA even possible under current law?"* The answer is yes. The **UN Charter's Article 22** provides the authority:

> "The General Assembly may establish such subsidiary organs as it deems necessary for the performance of its functions."

With a **two-thirds majority vote**, the UNGA could establish a Parliamentary Assembly tomorrow. It would not require Charter amendment or Security Council approval. The power already exists. What is missing is political will.

This is a crucial point: the General Assembly need not wait for permission. By Article 22, it can act. It only needs courage to claim the authority that conscience already gives it.

---

8. Call to Action

- **For Diplomats**: Table resolutions under Article 22 for the creation of a UN Parliamentary Assembly.

- **For National Parliaments**: Pass motions urging your governments to support a UNPA. Show that this is not utopian but practical.

- **For Civil Society**: Mobilise campaigns demanding global representation. Link climate, disarmament, and justice struggles to the need for a people's chamber.

- **For Citizens**: See yourself as a voter not only in your nation but in humanity. Demand the right to be represented at the global level.

Conclusion: Completing the Ladder

From local councils to county chambers, from devolved parliaments to Westminster, from Westminster to Europe - and beyond - the UK experience shows the logic of the Parliamentary Ladder. Disputes always grow wider, and parliaments always expand to meet them.

Now the disputes of humanity span the planet. They cannot be contained or solved by sovereignty alone. They require a global parliament.

The United Nations Parliamentary Assembly is not just an idea; it is the next rung on humanity's ladder. The UNGA already has the legal authority, under Article 22, to create it by a two-thirds majority.

The question is not whether we can, but whether we will. The ladder is before us. The next step is ours to take.

Chapter 7. Law-Making, Trust, and the Boundary of Harm

Introduction: Why Law Matters

At its best, law is humanity's way of preventing harm and enabling vitality. It gives shape to our shared life: providing safety, resolving disputes, expressing values, and creating predictability. It supports the essential humane life force, against an inhumane death force.

At best, law aims to build heaven on earth, to turn humanity away from the path to hell.

Without law, fear rules. Without predictability, trust collapses. Without trust, cooperation becomes impossible.

Yet law is not infallible. When it strays beyond its proper boundaries, it risks becoming arbitrary, eroding trust instead of building it. The most urgent example of this confusion lies in distinguishing between **objective harm** — the rightful domain of law — and **subjective offence** — which belongs to dialogue, not criminality.

1. The Purpose of Law-Making

The purpose of law is not simply to control behaviour. It is to:

- **Prevent harm** — shielding people from violence, exploitation, neglect, and systemic breakdown.

- **Resolve conflict** — replacing violence with structured processes.

- **Enable vitality** — creating conditions for flourishing through education, health, trade, and innovation.

- **Express shared values** — crystallising a society's conscience into standards.

- **Provide predictability** — reducing arbitrariness, building trust.

These purposes rest on a central truth: **law exists to weave predictability and conscience together into trust.**

---

2. Objective Harm: The Domain of Law

Objective harms are those that are:

- **Material**: physical, economic, environmental.

- **Evidential**: provable by witnesses, science, or agreed facts.

- **Predictable**: foreseeable to a reasonable person.

- **Systemic**: undermining of trust if unchecked.

Examples:

- Assault, theft, fraud.

- Building unsafe structures.

- Polluting rivers.

- Deploying weapons of mass destruction.

In all these cases, law's intervention is legitimate and essential.

---

3. Subjective Offence: The Domain of Dialogue

Subjective harms are real in experience but variable in meaning:

- One person is insulted; another laughs.

- A work of art offends one group; another celebrates it.

- Words or gestures wound in one culture but not in another.

These cannot be measured or predicted reliably. To criminalise them is to make law arbitrary:

- Citizens cannot know in advance what is unlawful.

- Policing shifts from protecting people to policing feelings.

- Trust collapses because law becomes capricious.

Principle: *Subjective offence belongs to dialogue, not criminality.* It requires education, culture, tolerance, and mediation — not police cells.

---

4. The Hybrid Zone: When Subjective Harm Becomes Objective

Some subjective harms cross into objective harm when they produce measurable, predictable damage:

- Sustained harassment → proven psychological injury.

- Incitement to violence → foreseeable physical harm.

- Systematic hate speech → documented exclusion or persecution.

Here, law is justified — but only when clear evidence shows the harm has moved from perception to predictable damage.

---

5. The Predictability Test

A simple test can anchor trust:

- **Could a reasonable person know in advance that this action would be unlawful?**

If yes → legitimate law.
If no → arbitrary law, eroding trust.

This test guards against the slide into criminalising "mere offence."

---

6. Implications for Global Governance

At the UN level, this boundary is critical:

- **Objective harms** — war, genocide, nuclear use, ecocide — demand binding law.

- **Subjective offences** — national insults, cultural slights, loss of face — must not be criminalised, or diplomacy would collapse.

- **Hybrid harms** — incitement to violence, systemic hate propaganda — can legitimately be addressed, but only with high evidential standards.

Without this clarity, international law risks being hijacked by those who weaponise offence for political ends.

---

7. Conscience as Guide

Law cannot stand alone. It must be guided by conscience to discern what rises to objective harm, what belongs to dialogue, and what crosses the threshold into systemic danger.

A UN Conscience Council would help clarify these boundaries. But the principle is universal: **law protects against real harm; dialogue absorbs offence.**

---

8. Call to Action

- **For Legislators**: Anchor laws in objective harm. Resist the drift into criminalising offence.

- **For Judges**: Apply the predictability test. Uphold fairness over arbitrariness.

- **For Citizens**: Defend free speech, but use dialogue to resolve offence.

- **For the UNGA**: Set standards that protect humanity from harm while preserving space for pluralism and tolerance.

Conclusion: The Boundary of Trust

The difference between objective harm and subjective offence is more than semantics. It is the boundary between law that builds trust and law that destroys it.

PATH to Peace - A Preventative Armistice Treaty for Humanity

If law is predictable, evidence-based, and rooted in conscience, it prevents harm and enables vitality. If law is arbitrary, swayed by offence, it creates fear and erodes legitimacy.

For humanity to rise into global trust, our laws must be clear: **Objective harm belongs to law. Subjective offence belongs to dialogue. Hybrid harms require evidence. Predictability is the anchor of trust.**

Only then can law fulfil its highest purpose: preventing harm, enabling vitality, and guiding humanity into peace.

Chapter 8. Witness Consciousness

Introduction: The Power of Presence

Conflict is fueled by noise: words sharpened into weapons, accusations hurled across borders, threats amplified through media. In this cacophony, what is missing is presence — the stillness that sees without judgment, that listens without fear, that holds space for truth to emerge.

This presence is what we call **witness consciousness**. It is not passive observation. It is active attention — the ability to stand in the heat of conflict without being consumed, to notice what is happening without reacting blindly, to hold open the possibility of transformation when others see only threat.

Witness consciousness is as old as humanity. It is the heart of spiritual practice, the foundation of peacemaking, the secret of effective coaching, and the missing ingredient in global governance. In this chapter, we explore how witness consciousness works, why it matters, and how it can change not only individual lives but the destiny of nations.

Wars are fuelled by reactivity and projection. Peace begins when someone stands in witness, holding the ability to observe without judgment, to step into shared bodymind space, to hold truth with presence. From Gandhi's quiet force to modern coaching methods, witness consciousness transforms conflict by revealing deeper reality.

Here, we trace how individual practice can ripple into global politics, turning meetings of leaders from defensive battlefields into spaces of recognition and humanity.

---

1. The Meaning of Witness

To witness is to see. Yet in the context of consciousness, witnessing is more than looking with the eyes. It is seeing with awareness. It is stepping back from identification with one side or another, and recognising the whole field.

Witness consciousness has three qualities:

1. **Non-reactivity**: It does not get hooked by provocation.

2. **Compassion**: It recognises the humanity of all sides, even the aggressor.

3. **Clarity**: It discerns patterns beneath the surface — the fears, shames, and needs that drive behaviour.

In personal life, witness consciousness allows us to see our own thoughts and emotions without being ruled by them. In politics, it allows leaders to step out of defensive posturing and notice the wider picture. In global governance, it allows institutions to transcend groupthink and act from conscience.

---

2. Witness in History

History offers glimpses of witness consciousness at work.

- **Gandhi** embodied it through nonviolent resistance. He saw the British Empire not as an enemy to be destroyed but as a system that could be transformed through truth and non-cooperation. His presence disarmed violence.

- **Martin Luther King Jr.** stood as witness in the face of racism. He did not return hatred with hatred. He held up a mirror to America, revealing its hypocrisy and inviting its conscience.

- **Nelson Mandela**, after decades in prison, could have emerged with bitterness. Instead, he chose reconciliation, seeing not only the pain of black South Africans but also the fear of whites. His witness consciousness birthed a new South Africa.

Each of these leaders did more than argue policies. They embodied presence. They revealed a deeper truth: that witness is itself a form of power.

---

3. Witness in Coaching and Dialogue

In modern coaching, witness consciousness is central. A good coach does not impose advice or judgment. They hold space, listening so deeply that the client hears their own truth emerging.

This is what happens when two or more are gathered in genuine dialogue: a third presence emerges, greater than either alone. The space itself becomes intelligent. New insights arise that neither party could have generated on their own.

At the diplomatic level, the same dynamic is possible. When leaders gather not merely to defend positions but to listen in witness, something shifts. The room itself becomes transformative. Agreements that seemed impossible suddenly appear obvious.

---

4. Witness and the Shared BodyMind

Witness consciousness is not just individual; it is relational. When we step into witness, we enter what can be called a **Shared BodyMind Space** — a field of awareness where truth already lives.

In this space, we sense not only our own perspective but the perspective of others. We feel what they feel, see what they see, without losing ourselves. It is as if a deeper intelligence connects us, whispering what needs to be known.

This is why witness consciousness is powerful in conflict resolution. It bypasses the masks of politics and touches the shared humanity beneath. In this space, adversaries can recognise themselves in each other.

---

5. Witness as Antidote to Groupthink

Groupthink thrives on unexamined assumptions, on fear of standing out, on conformity to power. Witness consciousness disrupts this.

In the UNGA, delegates often parrot lines scripted by ministries, repeating narratives without reflection. The result is paralysis. But if even a few delegates stood in witness — naming what they see without fear of ridicule — the group dynamic could shift.

Witness is contagious. One person willing to tell the truth calmly can open space for others to admit what they already know. This is how groupthink is broken: not by louder arguments, but by quieter presence.

6. Witness and Shame

Much of global conflict is driven by shame: the buried wounds of leaders, the humiliation of nations, the projection of weakness onto others. Witness consciousness allows shame to be acknowledged without judgment.

When shame is met with attack, it hardens into defensiveness. When shame is met with witness, it softens into vulnerability. Vulnerability, paradoxically, becomes the foundation of reconciliation.

Imagine a nuclear leader admitting before the UN: *"Yes, I fear humiliation. That is why we cling to these weapons."* If such an admission were met not with scorn but with witness, it could open the door to transformation.

7. Practicing Witness at All Levels

Witness is not only for saints or presidents. It is a practice for everyone.

- **In families**, witness means listening without interrupting, seeing beyond anger to the hurt beneath.

- **In workplaces**, it means noticing dynamics without rushing to blame, allowing truth to surface.

- **In communities**, it means holding dialogue circles where people speak and are heard.

- **In politics**, it means citizens refusing to demonise opponents, insisting on seeing their humanity.

At every level of governance — from rural councils to corporate boards to the UN — witness can be practiced. The higher the stakes, the greater the need.

---

8. Witness as Collective Power

Sovereignty belongs to states. Profit belongs to corporations. But witness belongs to peoples. It is the one power that cannot be monopolised by elites.

This is why mass movements often succeed where diplomacy fails. When millions stand in peaceful witness — as in the civil rights marches, the fall of the Berlin Wall, or climate protests today — governments are forced to respond. The sheer presence of people, nonviolent and unwavering, changes the field.

A global movement of witness, standing behind the UNGA as it confronts the WMD Villains, could embolden delegates to break free of groupthink. Witness is the people's veto on fear.

9. Toward a Witness Chamber

What if the UN itself institutionalised witness? What if, alongside the Security Council and the General Assembly, there was a **Witness Chamber** — a space where conscience, civil society, and citizens could testify without fear?

This is not far-fetched. Truth and Reconciliation Commissions after apartheid were forms of institutionalised witness. Hearings in parliaments often serve as spaces of witness. The International Criminal Court allows victims to testify.

A UN Witness Chamber could give voice to humanity directly — a conscience forum complementing the UN Parliamentary Assembly. Together, they would embody both structural authority and spiritual presence.

10. Call to Action

- **For Leaders**: Practice witness in meetings. Before reacting, breathe. Ask: *What is really being said beneath the words?*

- **For Diplomats**: Break groupthink by naming what you see with calm clarity. Trust that others already know it too.

- **For Citizens**: Practice witness in daily life. Refuse to dehumanise. Create spaces for dialogue.

- **For Movements**: Organise acts of collective witness — vigils, marches, testimonies — that embody presence more than protest.

Conclusion: The Eye of the Storm

The world today is like a storm: noise, violence, fear. Yet every storm has an eye — a still center where clarity reigns. Witness consciousness is that eye. It does not deny the storm, but it reveals another reality within it.

If leaders, diplomats, corporations, and citizens learned to live from witness, wars could be prevented, shame could be healed, and humanity could cross the Fear Gap together.

The PATH to Peace is not only treaties and institutions. It is also presence. Without witness, treaties collapse into words. With witness, even enemies can become allies.

The time has come to recover this ancient power, to practice it at every level, and to bring it into the heart of the United Nations. For in witness, humanity sees itself — and in seeing, becomes whole.

Chapter 9. Shared Humanity, Shared Shame

Introduction: The Hidden Emotion Behind Conflict

Fear is visible. We can see it in the tightening of muscles, the clenching of fists, the building of arsenals. But beneath fear lies another emotion, quieter and more corrosive: **shame**.

Shame is the hidden driver of human conflict. Nations humiliated in history cling to weapons for dignity. Leaders shamed in childhood wield power to mask their wounds. Peoples scarred by conquest or genocide project their pain outward in anger.

Yet shame is rarely named. It hides behind words like "honour," "security," or "sovereignty." It whispers in the silence after a defeat. It festers in the stories nations tell about themselves. Unacknowledged, it fuels cycles of projection and revenge.

But there is another way. When shame is recognised and shared, it becomes the doorway to reconciliation. Vulnerability, once feared, becomes strength. Acknowledged shame connects us to our **shared humanity**.

This chapter explores how shame operates in leaders, nations, and institutions — and how recognising it can transform conflict.

Beneath aggression lies buried shame. Many leaders carry childhood wounds of bullying, exclusion, or unmet love, which then project outward in the form of domination and war. This chapter names the hidden thread linking personal trauma to global violence.

It shows that shame, when denied, divides; but when acknowledged, it unites. The shared recognition of our own vulnerability — leaders and peoples alike — becomes the basis for reconciliation. This is not weakness, but the deepest source of strength and progress.

---

1. The Nature of Shame

Shame differs from guilt. Guilt says: *I did something wrong.* Shame says: *I am wrong.* Guilt focuses on actions; shame attacks identity.

At the personal level, shame arises when we feel unworthy, excluded, or dishonoured. Children who are bullied, belittled, or neglected carry wounds of shame into adulthood. Many leaders, beneath their public masks, carry these scars.

At the collective level, shame arises when nations are defeated, colonised, or disrespected. They respond by building myths of grandeur, clinging to weapons, or projecting humiliation onto enemies.

Shame's power lies in silence. What is not spoken festers. Leaders rarely admit shame, fearing it will be seen as weakness. Nations cover it with pride or aggression. Yet the unacknowledged wound shapes behaviour far more than most realise.

---

2. Childhood Shame, Adult Power

Behind the swagger of many world leaders lie stories of childhood shame.

- Some were bullied in schoolyards and vowed never to be humiliated again.

- Others grew up under harsh fathers or absent mothers, striving to prove themselves worthy.

- Still others experienced poverty or exclusion, carrying a wound of inferiority into positions of power.

These personal shames do not disappear when someone enters politics. They scale up. The schoolyard becomes the international stage. Rivals become enemies. Weapons become armour against old wounds.

The tragedy is that unhealed shame, when magnified by power, can endanger millions. A leader who cannot face personal vulnerability may choose war over compromise, annihilation over humility.

---

3. National Shame and Historical Wounds

Nations, too, carry shame. Consider:

- **Germany after World War I**: Humiliated by the Treaty of Versailles, it turned to nationalism and vengeance, paving the way for World War II.

- **Russia after the Cold War**: Shamed by the collapse of the Soviet Union, it clings to military might to restore lost dignity.

- **Japan after Hiroshima and Nagasaki**: Scarred by nuclear trauma, it lives in a paradox of victimhood and alliance with a nuclear power.

- **Colonised nations**: Many still carry the humiliation of exploitation, struggling to reclaim dignity on the world stage.

National shame often masquerades as pride. Military parades, nationalist slogans, and aggressive policies are sometimes less about strength than about covering old wounds.

---

4. Institutional Shame and the United Nations

Institutions also carry shame. The UN was founded "to save succeeding generations from the scourge of war," yet it has failed to prevent countless conflicts. The paralysis of the Security Council, the submission of the General Assembly, the impotence in the face of genocide — all these are sources of institutional shame.

Instead of admitting failure, institutions often retreat into procedure and rhetoric. Reports are written, resolutions passed, but the shame of powerlessness remains unspoken. This silence fuels cynicism, erodes legitimacy, and perpetuates groupthink.

Yet institutions, like people, can be healed by facing their shame. Imagine the UNGA openly acknowledging: *"We have failed to prevent war, but we now choose to rise to our true authority as the conscience of humanity."* Such honesty would not weaken the UN; it would renew it.

5. The Projection of Shame

Unacknowledged shame rarely stays hidden. It is projected outward.

- A leader shamed in youth humiliates opponents to avoid feeling small.

- A nation humiliated in history treats neighbours as threats.

- An institution embarrassed by failure scapegoats individuals or avoids responsibility.

Projection creates enemies where none need exist. It turns inner wounds into outer wars. The cycle is vicious: the more shame is denied, the more aggressively it is projected, and the more conflict escalates.

This is why nuclear deterrence is so dangerous. It is not only a strategy of fear; it is a projection of shame. Leaders terrified of appearing weak threaten annihilation instead. The world becomes hostage to their unhealed wounds.

6. The Courage to Admit Shame

The path of transformation begins with courage — the courage to admit shame.

- A leader who says, *"Yes, I fear humiliation. That is why we cling to weapons,"* is already freer than one who hides behind slogans.

- A nation that acknowledges historical wounds is already healing.

- An institution that confesses its failures is already renewing its legitimacy.

Admission disarms shame. What was poisonous in silence becomes powerful in honesty. Vulnerability invites empathy. Instead of ridicule, it evokes respect.

---

7. Shared Humanity, Shared Shame

Shame unites us because it is universal. Every person knows the sting of humiliation. Every nation has wounds. Every institution has failures.

To recognise this is to touch shared humanity. The leader who admits vulnerability speaks for all of us. The nation that acknowledges humiliation reflects the common human condition. The institution that confesses failure becomes relatable rather than remote.

Shared shame becomes the ground for reconciliation. When we admit that we all carry wounds, we can stop projecting and start healing.

---

8. Truth and Reconciliation as Witness to Shame

South Africa's Truth and Reconciliation Commission provides a model. Victims told their stories of humiliation and suffering. Perpetrators admitted their crimes. The nation bore witness. Shame, once buried, was brought into the light.

This did not erase pain, but it allowed healing. The process was imperfect, but it showed that public acknowledgement of shame can prevent cycles of revenge.

Imagine a global equivalent — a **Truth and Humanity Commission** — where nations could confess historical wounds and humiliations, not to be judged but to be witnessed. Such a chamber could release tensions that otherwise explode into violence.

---

9. The UNGA's Role in Breaking the Cycle

The UNGA must also confront its shame. It has too often bowed to the Security Council, believing itself powerless. This submissive posture is itself a form of shame — internalised humiliation before the P5.

But the TPNW shows that conscience is already in the majority. The UNGA has the power to stand up to the bullies. Its own path from shame to courage mirrors the journey leaders and nations must take.

By admitting its failures and asserting its conscience, the General Assembly can transform its shame into authority. It can become the chamber where humanity's wounds are acknowledged and healed.

---

10. Call to Action

- **For Leaders**: Admit vulnerability. Speak honestly about fears of humiliation. You will gain respect, not lose it.

- **For Nations**: Confront historical wounds. Teach them, not to fuel vengeance, but to foster reconciliation.

- **For Institutions**: Name your failures openly. Use them as stepping stones to legitimacy.

- **For Citizens**: Share your own shame stories. Create cultures where vulnerability is honoured, not mocked.

- **For the UNGA**: Stand up to the WMD Villains. Take the TPNW forward. Lead humanity out of the cycle of humiliation.

Conclusion: The Doorway to Reconciliation

Shame is the hidden emotion that fuels war. Left unacknowledged, it projects outward as aggression. But admitted and shared, it becomes the doorway to reconciliation.

We are all wounded. Leaders, nations, institutions — none are exempt. But in that shared shame lies our shared humanity. By admitting it, we can stop projecting, stop escalating, and start healing.

The PATH to Peace requires treaties, parliaments, and conscience. But it also requires vulnerability. Only by facing our shame together can we rise into the wholeness of humanity.

Chapter 10. Preventative Armistice — The PATH to Peace

Introduction: Every War Ends in a Treaty

Every war ends the same way: not with total victory, not with annihilation, but with a **treaty**. Men and women sit around tables, exhausted by bloodshed, and finally agree to terms. Land is divided, reparations assigned, promises written. The war that once seemed unstoppable ends with words on paper.

But here lies the tragic absurdity: humanity insists on fighting wars to exhaustion before signing the agreements that could have been reached at the start. Millions die, cities are destroyed, generations scarred — and then the peace table produces what was always possible.

This chapter argues for a different path: a **Preventative Armistice Treaty of Humanity (PATH)**. Instead of waiting for World War III to devastate civilisation, we must agree now on the standards and structures that would inevitably follow such a catastrophe. We must sign the peace treaty before the war begins.

The PATH to Peace is framed as common sense: we either sign now, in foresight, or sign later in regret. The decision is urgent.

1. Learning from Aviation: Managing Risk Dispassionately

The aviation industry once faced catastrophic risks. Aircraft crashed with terrifying regularity. Every accident threatened public confidence. The response could have been fear, secrecy, and blame. Instead, aviation pioneered a different model: **confidential reporting systems**.

Pilots, engineers, and staff were encouraged to report mistakes, near-misses, and hazards anonymously. The focus was not punishment but learning. Patterns were identified, systemic flaws corrected, training improved. The result: aviation became one of the safest industries in the world.

This model is precisely what global security requires. At present, nations treat mistakes as shameful secrets. Nuclear near-misses are covered up. Leaders posture as infallible. Fear of humiliation prevents honesty. But if humanity adopted a **confidential, dispassionate system of risk reporting**, much like aviation's, many dangers could be averted.

Imagine a global body where states could admit errors — missile misfires, cyber intrusions, doctrinal confusions — without ridicule or sanction, but with the aim of prevention. Such a system would transform nuclear risk management from blame to learning. It would allow the world to address dangers before they become disasters.

The Preventative Armistice Treaty should include such mechanisms. Just as aviation recognises that safety is everyone's business, so too must humanity recognise that survival is our shared responsibility.

---

2. The Folly of Waiting

History is littered with examples of wars that could have been prevented by foresight.

- **World War I**: Diplomats stumbled into catastrophe through alliances and pride. Millions died, only for borders to be redrawn in ways that could have been negotiated beforehand.

- **World War II**: The failure to address Germany's humiliation after Versailles made war almost inevitable. The post-war settlement, with the UN and European cooperation, could have been established earlier and spared devastation.

- **The Cold War**: For decades, humanity lived on the knife-edge of nuclear annihilation. Eventually, arms control treaties and dialogue reduced tensions — agreements that could have been reached without decades of fear.

The lesson is stark: peace treaties are not post-war luxuries. They are pre-war necessities. The choice is not between signing or not signing, but between signing before catastrophe or after.

---

3. What a Preventative Armistice Means

A **Preventative Armistice Treaty of Humanity** would not be just another document. It would be a framework for avoiding the war that everyone fears yet no one can win.

Its principles might include:

PATH to Peace - A Preventative Armistice Treaty for Humanity

1. **No First Use of Nuclear Weapons**: A universal pledge to remove the hair-trigger of annihilation.

2. **Phased Nuclear Disarmament**: A timeline for reducing arsenals under international verification.

3. **Confidential Risk Reporting**: A system modelled on aviation safety, encouraging honesty and learning.

4. **Strengthened UNGA Role**: Recognition that the General Assembly, not the Security Council, is the true conscience of humanity.

5. **Institution of a Conscience Council**: A body to evaluate decisions against humanity's survival and dignity.

6. **Pathway to a UN Parliamentary Assembly**: Institutionalising people-power as a chamber of humanity.

7. **Commitment to Nonviolent Dispute Resolution**: Making parliamentary debate, not armed conflict, the norm.

Such a treaty would be humanity's **PATH to Peace** — a preventative structure that addresses root risks before they explode.

---

4. Why Prevention Is Hard

If prevention is so obvious, why does humanity resist it? Three reasons dominate:

- **Addiction to Power**: Leaders cling to weapons as symbols of dignity, even when they know the risks. (We will return to this addiction in the 12-step framework later in the book.)

- **Fear of Humiliation**: Nations dread appearing weak by signing agreements before war, mistaking foresight for surrender.

- **Groupthink**: Institutions assume war is inevitable, focusing only on management rather than prevention.

These obstacles are psychological, not practical. They can be overcome once leaders and peoples recognise that prevention is not weakness but wisdom.

---

5. The Role of the UNGA

The UN General Assembly is the natural forum to birth the Preventative Armistice Treaty. The Security Council, dominated by the WMD Villains, cannot lead. Its members profit from fear. But the General Assembly, where conscience is already in the majority, can act.

Under **Article 22 of the UN Charter**, the UNGA can establish subsidiary bodies necessary for its functions. With a two-thirds majority, it could establish a process to draft and adopt the PATH to Peace. The TPNW shows the precedent: a treaty born in the First Committee, championed by conscience, carried by the majority.

The Preventative Armistice would be the next step — a treaty that binds humanity not after the catastrophe, but before.

---

6. How the PATH Differs from Past Treaties

Past arms control agreements have been about **managing rivalry**. SALT, START, INF — all were negotiated in the shadow of fear, designed to balance power rather than transcend it.

The PATH would be different. It would not emerge from rivalry but from recognition of shared survival. Its logic would not be deterrence but conscience. Its aim would not be to perpetuate the status quo but to transform it.

This is why the aviation analogy matters. Past treaties punished error. The PATH would encourage honesty. Past treaties froze power. The PATH would release humanity.

---

7. The Practical Steps

How could such a treaty be born?

1. **Mobilise the Majority**: Nations that signed the TPNW must lead, reminding the UNGA that conscience is already the majority.

2. **Launch a First Committee Process**: Begin drafting the treaty as an extension of disarmament and security work.

3. **Embed Confidential Risk Reporting**: Create systems for near-miss disclosure, anonymous reporting, and shared analysis.

4. **Build Civil Society Support**: NGOs, faith groups, and influencers must campaign for prevention, not just protest after war.

5. **Invite Leaders to Heroism**: The WMD Villains must be offered a role in shaping the PATH, not as shameful offenders but as potential heroes.

---

8. Overcoming Resistance

Resistance will be fierce. The WMD Villains will claim the PATH undermines deterrence. Critics will scoff that prevention is naïve. But resistance can be disarmed by reframing:

- Prevention is not surrender; it is foresight.

- Confidential reporting is not weakness; it is wisdom.

- Conscience is not utopian; it is practical survival.

The aviation industry transformed itself by embracing these truths. So can global governance.

---

9. Call to Action

- **For Diplomats**: Table resolutions for a Preventative Armistice Treaty. Use Article 22 to create the drafting body.

- **For Nations**: Join the process, whether or not you are nuclear-armed. The treaty protects all.

- **For Civil Society**: Launch campaigns demanding foresight. Use aviation analogies to show prevention works.

- **For Citizens**: Ask your leaders: *Why must we wait for war before we sign peace?*

- **For Influencers**: Create narratives — films, stories, media — showing the absurdity of post-war treaties and the wisdom of pre-war ones.

Conclusion: The PATH Before Us

Every war ends with a treaty. The only question is when. Will we wait until after cities burn and millions die, or will we act now?

The Preventative Armistice Treaty of Humanity is not a dream. It is the only logical step for a species that has outgrown war. Aviation proved that risks can be managed dispassionately, through honesty and shared learning. Humanity must do the same.

The PATH to Peace is before us. It is a path we can walk now, before catastrophe forces our hand. The choice is ours — foresight or regret, prevention or destruction, life or death.

Chapter 11. The End of the Need for War

Introduction: Questioning the Old Assumption

For as long as history has been recorded, war has been treated as inevitable. From the earliest chronicles of kings and empires to the modern doctrines of national defence, the assumption is the same: there will always be enemies, there will always be battles, there will always be war.

This assumption is so deeply embedded that few dare to question it. Academics call it "human nature." Politicians call it "realism." Military planners call it "preparedness." But beneath the language lies the same fatalistic belief: war is permanent, peace is temporary.

This chapter challenges that assumption. It argues that war is not written into human DNA. War is a cultural practice, a product of outdated vows, traumas, and addictions. Conflict is natural — but **the need for war is not**. Humanity can learn to resolve disputes without violence, just as we once learned to abolish slavery, outlaw duels, and ban human sacrifice.

The time has come to declare that the age of war is over — not because conflict disappears, but because humanity has outgrown the need to resolve it through destruction. Put simply: war no longer *works*.

It is now understood that the purpose of conflict is to force people to work together to raise their understanding to a new level, by means of insight through dialogue, leading to the goal of a change of common perspective. That is the transformation process.

This chapter challenges the deepest myth of human nature: that violence is necessary. It argues instead that conflict is natural, but war is not. Humanity can outgrow the need for war by shifting perspective, by learning to resolve disputes through conscience and cooperation. This is not utopia, but the next stage of maturity.

---

1. War as Humanity's Oldest Addiction

War functions like an addiction. Nations return to it despite the damage, justifying it with illusions of honour, security, or necessity. Leaders escalate conflicts even when alternatives exist. Citizens rally around flags even as their lives are ruined.

Like all addictions, war offers short-term relief — a sense of power, unity, or vindication. But it creates long-term devastation: death, displacement, economic ruin, psychological trauma.

Addictions thrive on denial. Just as an addict insists, "I can stop anytime," nations insist, "This war is necessary." Just as addicts blame others for their cravings, nations blame enemies for their violence.

Humanity's addiction to war has lasted millennia. But as with other addictions, recovery begins with recognition: to admit that war is not a need, but a destructive habit we can leave behind.

---

2. The Vow of "Never Again" and Its Paradox

After every great war, humanity has sworn "Never again." After World War I, this vow produced the League of Nations. After World War II, it produced the United Nations. After Hiroshima and Nagasaki, it produced the NPT and disarmament treaties.

Yet paradoxically, the vow of "Never again" often drives preparation for the next war. In fear of repetition, nations arm themselves to the teeth. Holocaust trauma drives nuclear buildup. Post-colonial trauma fuels military nationalism. The vow becomes its opposite: *We must be so strong that it never happens again.* And in striving to prevent it, we recreate it.

This is the paradox of trauma-driven vows. They bind us to the very cycle we wish to escape. The only way out is transformation: to change perspective, to see that true security lies not in arms but in conscience and cooperation.

---

3. The Economic Illusion of War

Another reason war persists is the illusion that it sustains economies. Weapons industries employ millions. Military budgets drive research. Politicians fear unemployment if arms production ceases.

But this too is illusion. War is not wealth; it is waste. The same resources poured into weapons could build renewable energy, cure diseases, or provide education. Every bomb is a school not built, a hospital not staffed, a field not planted.

Economists increasingly recognise that war spending distorts economies, creating dependence on destruction. Peace economies, by contrast, generate sustainable prosperity. The transition is not easy, but it is possible — as many industries that shifted from wartime to peacetime production after 1945 proved.

The Preventative Armistice Treaty would include not just disarmament clauses but pathways for economic conversion: turning weapons industries into engines of welfare.

---

4. War as a Failure of Imagination

At root, war persists because humanity has failed to imagine alternatives. Leaders see only two options: surrender or fight. Citizens are told the same story: without war, enemies will destroy us.

But imagination creates reality. The abolition of slavery once seemed impossible. Women's suffrage once seemed absurd. Ending war will seem equally impossible until we imagine it, and then act.

The UN Parliamentary Assembly, the Conscience Council, and the Preventative Armistice are all exercises in imagination. They show that alternatives exist. They remind us that war is not destiny, but choice: a choice of perspective.

---

5. From "Just War" to "Just Peace"

For centuries, philosophers developed theories of "just war" — conditions under which violence could be morally justified. These frameworks gave legitimacy to countless conflicts.

Now the time has come to replace "just war" with **"just peace."** Instead of debating when war is permissible, humanity must debate how peace can be preserved. The guiding question must change from *"When may we kill?"* to *"How shall we live?"*

"Just peace" is not naïve. It recognises conflict but insists it be channelled into parliaments, courts, and councils. It sets standards: peace must be fair, inclusive, and sustainable. It demands conscience at every level.

---

6. War and the Fear Gap

The persistence of war is also tied to the **Fear Gap**. Leaders fear humiliation more than destruction. Nations fear weakness more than annihilation. In resisting shame, they provoke the very wars they dread.

The Fear Gap explains why deterrence doctrines persist even when they risk mutual annihilation. Leaders would rather gamble with survival than admit vulnerability.

But as we saw earlier, crossing the Fear Gap is possible. It requires courage, reframing, and conscience. Once crossed, the "need" for war dissolves, revealed as illusion.

---

7. The Role of Witness in Ending War

Witness consciousness, explored in the previous chapter, is essential here. Ending war requires more than treaties; it requires new ways of seeing. When peoples and leaders witness their own shame and fear without judgment, they can imagine alternatives.

Truth commissions, reconciliation processes, and nonviolent movements all prove the point: witnessing transforms conflict. The end of war will come not through conquest but through presence.

---

8. The Steps Toward Ending War

To declare the end of war is bold. But boldness must be matched by steps. The pathway includes:

1. **Naming War as Addiction**: Admitting the cycle, recognising its destructiveness.

2. **Building Alternatives**: Strengthening parliaments, councils, and assemblies at every level.

3. **Economic Conversion**: Redirecting military industries toward welfare.

4. **Cultural Transformation**: Creating narratives where peace is heroic, war is obsolete.

5. **Legal Prohibition**: Expanding treaties like the TPNW into broader bans on war itself.

Each step builds on the last, weaving prevention, imagination, and conscience into a new normal.

---

9. Preparing the 12-Step Pathway

Later in this book, we will explore in detail a **12-step pathway out of addiction** — not to alcohol or drugs, but to power and war. Like all addicts, humanity must admit its problem, surrender control, seek help, make amends, and commit to change.

The 12-step framework offers more than metaphor. It is a practical structure for recovery. Leaders and peoples alike can walk it, transforming cycles of destruction into cycles of healing.

This chapter prepares the ground. By naming war as addiction, we set the stage for recovery. By admitting we no longer need war, we make space for a new future.

---

10. Call to Action

- **For Leaders**: Admit that war is not inevitable. Speak of peace as the new normal. Begin economic and institutional conversion.

- **For Diplomats**: Table resolutions that reframe security around prevention, not deterrence. Use the PATH treaty as leverage.

- **For Citizens**: Challenge the fatalism of "war is human nature." Share stories of peace, not only of conflict.

- **For Educators and Influencers**: Teach the history of human progress as a series of endings — of slavery, of duels, of colonialism — so that ending war feels possible.

- **For the UNGA**: Lead the declaration: "Humanity no longer needs war." Make it the guiding principle of the twenty-first century.

Conclusion: Declaring the End

Slavery ended. Duels ended. Human sacrifice ended. Each once seemed inevitable. Each is now unthinkable.

So it will be with war. The time has come to declare that humanity no longer needs it. Conflict will remain, but war — organised violence between peoples — can and must end.

The Preventative Armistice Treaty of Humanity will codify this shift. The Conscience Council will guide it. The UN Parliamentary Assembly will embody it. But the deepest step is within us: to recognise that war is not our destiny, but our addiction — and that we are ready to recover.

This is the turning point. From warfare to welfare, from violence to conscience, from addiction to freedom. The end of war is not a dream. It is the next step in humanity's awakening.

Chapter 12. Enlightened Leadership

Introduction: The Leaders We Have vs. The Leaders We Need

Humanity is not short of leaders. Presidents, prime ministers, CEOs, generals — the world is full of people in positions of authority. Yet the crises we face reveal a stark truth: the leaders we have are rarely the leaders we need.

Most current leaders are trapped in outdated paradigms — sovereignty, domination, deterrence. They manage appearances, chase popularity, protect power. But they rarely serve humanity as a whole. The result is paralysis at best, catastrophe at worst.

What humanity needs now is **enlightened leadership**. Not perfect leadership — no one is flawless — but integrated leadership. Leadership that draws on head, heart, and conscience. Leadership that embodies witness presence, acknowledges shame, and acts from purpose. Leadership that no longer hides behind fear but dares to serve humanity.

Enlightened leadership means wholeness: the capacity to hold fear, power, and conscience together in service. This chapter explores what it means for a leader to act as Guide, Elder, or Truthfinder — embodying presence without needing domination. Enlightened leadership is contagious; it inspires others to rise. Humanity's survival may depend less on weapons than on the cultivation of this kind of leader.

This chapter explores what enlightened leadership means, why it is urgently required, and how it can be cultivated.

---

1. What Enlightenment Is — and Is Not

The word "enlightenment" often evokes mysticism, halos, or perfection. But here, enlightenment means something simpler and more practical: **integration**.

- It is not the absence of flaws, but the ability to hold flaws honestly.

- It is not superhuman charisma, but the capacity to stand in presence.

- It is not private illumination, but public service.

Enlightened leadership is the integration of inner truth with outer responsibility. It is the willingness to see beyond narrow interests into the wider needs of humanity. It is not about being *above* others, but about being *with* others — as guide, witness, and servant.

---

2. The Shadow of Fear-Based Leadership

Most leaders today operate from fear, mostly unconscious. Fear of losing power. Fear of humiliation. Fear of enemies. Fear of change. This fear drives defensive policies, secrecy, and aggression.

Fear-based leadership creates cycles of violence. Leaders cling to weapons, escalate rivalries, and project their shame onto others. They believe they are protecting their nations, but in reality, they are perpetuating insecurity.

The tragedy is that fear-based leaders are often unaware of their own fear. They mask it with bravado, slogans, and threats. Yet beneath the surface lies the wound — the shame unacknowledged, the fear unexamined.

---

3. The Turn to Humanity

The transformation begins with a **turn** — a shift of perspective from self to service, from domination to humanity. This is the essence of enlightened leadership: to turn from fear into conscience, from rivalry into cooperation, from narrow sovereignty into shared responsibility.

This turn is not theoretical. It is practical, visible in choices:

- A leader admits vulnerability instead of posturing strength.

- A government signs disarmament treaties instead of escalating arsenals.

- A corporation invests in welfare instead of exploiting fear.

The turn is also contagious. When one leader dares to stand for humanity, others feel permission to follow. This is how villains become heroes — by choosing service over shame.

---

4. The Powers of Attention and Intention

Enlightened leadership requires mastery of two inner powers: **attention** and **intention**.

- **Attention**: the capacity to see clearly, to notice without distortion, to witness without being trapped in reaction.

- **Intention**: the capacity to act with clarity, to choose consciously, to articulate a vision, serve a higher purpose with higher values and standards - and set that direction.

Most leaders are scattered in attention and fragmented in intention. They chase headlines, react to crises, protect egos. Enlightened leaders cultivate focused attention and integrated intention. They hold the whole picture in awareness and choose actions aligned with conscience.

Together, attention and intention form the inner compass of enlightened leadership.

---

5. The Role of Witness Consciousness

Witness consciousness, explored earlier, is the foundation of enlightened leadership.

Leaders who can stand in presence — seeing fear, shame, and projection without reacting blindly — are leaders who can guide transformation.

Witness leadership disarms groupthink. It opens space for truth-telling. It models calm in crisis. It listens deeply to the voice of humanity itself.

In a world addicted to performance and power, witness leaders embody stillness. Their presence is itself transformative.

---

6. Conscience as Compass

Enlightened leaders use conscience as their compass. They ask not only, *What is possible?* or *What is popular?* but *What is right?*

Conscience is what prevents power from becoming abuse, strategy from becoming cruelty, policy from becoming betrayal. It expands vision beyond the present into the future, beyond one nation into humanity.

The TPNW nations already showed this kind of leadership. They acted not for narrow gain but for global survival. They demonstrated that conscience-led leadership is not utopian but practical.

---

7. The Courage to Admit Shame

A defining feature of enlightened leadership is the courage to admit shame. Leaders who confess vulnerability — who say, *Yes, I fear humiliation* — disarm conflict. Instead of escalating, they invite empathy.

This courage is revolutionary. In a world where leaders are trained to mask weakness, honesty becomes strength. Vulnerability becomes power.

Imagine a nuclear leader standing before the UNGA and admitting: *"We keep these weapons because we fear shame. But today, we choose humanity over fear."* Such words could change history.

---

8. The Addiction to Power

The greatest obstacle to enlightened leadership is addiction — to power, to control, to weapons. Like all addictions, it thrives on denial. Leaders insist they need weapons, just as addicts insist they need their substance.

Enlightened leadership recognises this addiction and chooses recovery. It acknowledges that true strength lies not in domination but in service. Later, in Chapter 12, we will map a **12-step pathway out of this addiction**, offering leaders a structure for recovery.

---

9. Cultivating Enlightened Leaders

How can we cultivate enlightened leaders? Several practices are essential:

1. **Mentorship and Coaching**: Leaders need guides who hold them accountable to conscience, not just strategy.

2. **Spiritual Practice**: Meditation, reflection, prayer — practices that cultivate witness presence and humility.

3. **Truth-Telling Circles**: Forums where leaders can speak honestly, admit vulnerability, and be witnessed without ridicule.

4. **Education in Conscience**: Training future leaders to see beyond narrow interests into humanity's needs.

Enlightenment is not an accident. It is a practice that can be nurtured.

---

10. Call to Action

- **For Leaders**: Practice presence. Admit vulnerability. Let conscience guide decisions.

- **For Diplomats**: Support leaders who embody conscience. Create spaces for truth, not just negotiation.

- **For Citizens**: Demand leaders who serve humanity, not ego. Celebrate vulnerability as strength.

- **For Movements**: Train leaders in witness consciousness and conscience. Make enlightenment a norm, not an exception.

- **For the UNGA**: Elevate leaders who embody conscience into positions of influence. Resist the groupthink that rewards only power.

Conclusion: The Leaders of Tomorrow

The leaders humanity needs are not supermen or saints. They are ordinary people who have chosen integration over fragmentation, conscience over fear, service over ego.

Enlightened leadership does not mean perfection. It means presence. It means courage. It means choosing humanity as the horizon of decision.

The world is waiting for such leaders. The stage is set. The crises are urgent. What remains is the choice: will today's leaders cling to addiction and fear, or will they turn to humanity and become heroes?

The PATH to Peace depends on this choice. Enlightened leadership is not a luxury. It is survival. And it is the destiny of those who dare to guide humanity from warfare to welfare.

Chapter 13. Enforcement Without War

Introduction: The Objection We Cannot Ignore

Every time a new treaty, institution, or vision for peace is proposed, sceptics ask the same question: *"But how will you enforce it?"*

It is a fair question. Without enforcement, agreements risk becoming words on paper. The WMD Villains themselves raise it cynically: *"Nice ideals, but who will make us comply?"* If we cannot answer, they will dismiss the PATH to Peace as naïve.

This chapter faces the objection squarely. It shows that enforcement is possible — but it must be understood differently. Enforcement cannot mean more armies, weapons, or bullying. That approach merely recreates the very addiction we are trying to end. Instead, enforcement must be built on legitimacy, verification, incentives, conscience, and education.

---

1. Legitimacy as Enforcement

The strongest force in human affairs is not coercion but **legitimacy**. When the majority of peoples and nations declare something unacceptable, even the most powerful outliers find compliance unavoidable.

- Slavery ended not because every slaveholder was overpowered, but because the moral norm shifted.

- Colonialism collapsed because its legitimacy eroded.

- Apartheid ended when global conscience refused to tolerate it.

So it will be with war and WMDs. Once the UNGA and "We the Peoples" declare their abolition, legitimacy itself becomes the enforcer.

---

2. Verification and Transparency

Legitimacy must be matched with trust. That is why the PATH to Peace includes rigorous **verification systems**, modelled on successful regimes:

- **Aviation Confidential Reporting Systems** show how dispassionate reporting of risks saves lives. Pilots admit errors without fear of punishment, knowing honesty prevents catastrophe. Nations can do the same with military risks.

- **Nuclear inspection regimes** already exist under the IAEA. These can be expanded and strengthened, with new technologies for monitoring and data-sharing.

- **Transparency** becomes a deterrent. Exposure of violations carries reputational costs greater than silence.

Enforcement, then, is less about punishment than about creating systems where honesty and visibility are safer than secrecy.

---

3. Incentives and Withdrawal of Privilege

Nations are motivated not only by fear but by gain. Enforcement works best when compliance brings rewards and violations bring the loss of privileges.

- Access to trade, finance, and technology can be linked to treaty adherence.

- Membership in a UN Parliamentary Assembly or Conscience Council can be restricted to compliant nations.

- Non-compliance isolates violators, stripping them of legitimacy and opportunity.

The message is simple: join humanity's future and prosper; resist, and face exclusion.

---

4. Precedent: Peaceful Resolution in History

Sceptics claim peace cannot be enforced. But history shows otherwise:

- **Cuban Missile Crisis**: Dialogue, back-channels, and statesmanship prevented annihilation.

- **Berlin Wall**: Restraint allowed peaceful collapse rather than bloodshed.

- **Good Friday Agreement**: Centuries of violence ended with negotiation.

- **South Africa**: Apartheid dissolved through truth and reconciliation, not civil war.

- **Hostage Negotiation**: On the micro scale, de-escalation and empathy resolve deadly crises daily.

These are not theories. They are precedents. Enforcement by dialogue, restraint, and dignity has already worked. The problem is not possibility, but will.

---

5. Breaking the Bully Dynamic

Today's villains persist because they are protected by bigger bullies. Regional tyrants know they can count on great-power backing. The P5 themselves are the archetypal bullies, defending their own weapons while condemning others.

Enforcement means **breaking this protection racket**. When the UNGA stands up to the P5, when citizens expose hypocrisy, when conscience strips away legitimacy, bullies are left naked. Without protection, smaller villains lose their impunity.

---

6. Education and Training: Preventing Bullies at the Source

The deepest enforcement is prevention: **ensuring bullies never rise to power in the first place.**

Right now, elections reward dominance, slogans, and fear. If we vote for bullies, we get bullies — and wars.

The answer is education:

- **Global Leadership Academies** to train leaders in conscience, witness presence, conflict transformation, and shame awareness.

- **Citizenship education** to help societies value humility and service over aggression.

- **Conflict-resolution training** in schools, corporations, and parliaments.

Enforcement is not just catching violators — it is **cultivating the right kind of leaders and citizens** so violation becomes less likely.

---

7. Enforcement Through Recovery Culture

Traditional enforcement punishes violators. But punishment is dangerous when dealing with nuclear powers. Instead, enforcement must mirror **addiction recovery**:

- Admit wrongs.

- Confess openly.

- Make amends.

- Re-join the community.

This creates a culture where nations can step back from violations without humiliation, restoring trust rather than escalating fear.

---

8. From Groupthink to Conscience

The UNGA must also change its own culture. Groupthink makes it grovel to the Security Council, convinced it is powerless. Enforcement will never work under this mindset.

But the TPNW shows conscience is already in the majority. The UNGA can enforce by standing firm, declaring: *"We are humanity's conscience. We no longer submit to the veto of bullies."*

---

9. Call to Action

- **For Leaders**: Accept verification. Welcome transparency. Lead by example.

- **For Diplomats**: Embed incentives and privileges into treaties. Make compliance rewarding.

- **For Citizens**: Refuse to elect bullies. Demand leaders who embody conscience.

- **For Educators**: Train the next generation in conflict transformation.

- **For the UNGA**: Break the bully dynamic. Enforce not with weapons, but with legitimacy and conscience.

Conclusion: Enforcement Without War

Enforcement does not mean more armies. It means **more humanity**. It means legitimacy as authority, transparency as deterrent, incentives as leverage, education as prevention, and recovery culture as healing.

History proves it can be done. The Cuban Missile Crisis, the Berlin Wall, Ireland, South Africa — all remind us: peace can be enforced by restraint, dignity, and courage.

The PATH to Peace does not dodge the enforcement question. It answers it: we enforce not through fear, but through conscience. Not through weapons, but through witness. Not through bullies, but through humanity.

This is enforcement without war.

Chapter 14. Governance of Humanity, by Humanity, for Humanity, with Humanity

Introduction: The Fulfilment of a Promise

When the United Nations was founded, its Charter began with words of astonishing clarity: *"We the Peoples of the United Nations, determined to save succeeding generations from the scourge of war ..."*

Those words remain the most profound promise humanity has ever written. Yet in practice, governance of the UN has been shaped less by "We the Peoples" than by "We the Powers." The P5, with their vetoes and weapons, have dominated. The General Assembly has too often submitted.

But the crises of our time make one truth unavoidable: governance must evolve. It must no longer be governance of humanity by elites, but governance of humanity **by humanity, for humanity, with humanity**. This chapter explores what that means — and how we can walk the recovery path out of our collective addiction to war.

PATH to Peace - A Preventative Armistice Treaty for Humanity

1. The Age of Impunity

We live in an **Age of Impunity**. Powerful nations act without accountability, shielded by vetoes and nuclear arsenals. Corporations manipulate law for profit. Institutions fail yet refuse to admit shame. Citizens feel powerless, alienated from decision-making.

This is unsustainable. Just as absolute monarchy gave way to parliaments, so too must impunity give way to conscience. Humanity cannot survive a future where the few hold weapons that can annihilate the many.

Governance must be re-founded on legitimacy, conscience, and shared responsibility.

---

2. The Conscience Council and UNPA

Two institutional reforms are pivotal:

- A **Conscience Council** within the UN, charged with testing all decisions against the standards of humanity's survival and dignity.

- A **UN Parliamentary Assembly**, created under Article 22, giving voice to citizens and parliaments, not just governments.

Together, these bodies would anchor governance in conscience and people-power. They would ensure that decisions reflect humanity as a whole, not just states or elites.

---

3. From Sovereignty to Stewardship

Sovereignty was a temporary fix after Westphalia. It helped end Europe's wars, but it is outdated in an interconnected world. We must now shift from sovereignty to **stewardship**.

- Sovereignty says: *This is mine; I control it.*

- Stewardship says: *This is ours; we care for it together.*

Stewardship is the essence of governance by humanity, for humanity, with humanity. It recognises that we share one planet, one atmosphere, one future.

---

4. Governance as Recovery

But how do we get there? The truth is sobering: humanity is addicted to war and power. Like addicts, we return to destructive habits even when they destroy us. We justify, we deny, we blame.

That is why governance reform cannot be only institutional. It must also be **psychological and spiritual**. We must treat our addiction as addiction, and walk a path of recovery.

The 12-step pathway, adapted from the recovery movement, offers a profound guide. It has helped millions escape cycles of denial and destruction. It can help humanity do the same with war.

---

5. The 12-Step Pathway Out of Addiction to War

PATH to Peace - A Preventative Armistice Treaty for Humanity

Here is how the classic steps translate into humanity's recovery:

1. **Admit Powerlessness**: Acknowledge that war is destroying us, and we are powerless if we cling to it.

2. **Recognise Higher Power**: Not a deity imposed, but the higher authority of conscience, humanity, and future generations.

3. **Surrender Control**: Accept that domination and sovereignty cannot save us. We must yield to shared stewardship.

4. **Take a Fearless Inventory**: Nations and leaders must examine their motives, wounds, and projections of shame.

5. **Confess Wrongs**: Admit openly — to one another and to humanity — the harms caused by war, weapons, and domination.

6. **Be Ready for Change**: Cultivate willingness to let go of weapons, pride, and addiction to power.

7. **Ask for Transformation**: Appeal not to pride but to conscience, to be lifted into a higher way of being.

8. **Make Amends**: Nations must repair the damage caused — to victims, to the planet, to humanity's trust.

9. **Direct Reconciliation**: Wherever possible, make peace directly with those harmed. Seek reconciliation rather than denial.

10. **Continue Self-Examination**: Governance must include constant conscience-auditing, reviewing motives and actions.

11. **Deepen Through Witness**: Practice presence, reflection, meditation — disciplines that anchor leaders in witness consciousness.

12. **Carry the Message**: Share the path of peace with others. Become role models for humanity.

These steps are not abstract. They can be embodied in institutions, policies, and personal practices. They turn governance into a recovery programme for civilisation.

---

6. Applying the Steps to Governance

- **At the UNGA**: Step 1 means admitting failure to prevent war. Step 2 means recognising conscience as higher authority. Step 3 means rejecting submission to the Security Council.

- **For Nations**: Step 8 means reparations, truth commissions, and reconciliation processes. Step 9 means disarmament and apologies.

- **For Corporations**: Step 10 means constant ethical audits. Step 11 means embedding conscience in boardrooms.

- **For Citizens**: Step 12 means carrying the message — becoming educators, influencers, and witnesses.

The recovery model gives governance a rhythm of humility, accountability, and renewal.

---

7. Groupthink vs. Recovery Culture

Groupthink denies problems, hides shame, and enforces conformity. Recovery culture admits problems, shares shame, and supports transformation.

The UNGA must move from groupthink to recovery. It must stop parroting the P5's myths of power and start admitting the truth: war is unsustainable, sovereignty is outdated, conscience is supreme.

The 12-step framework provides a language and practice for this cultural shift.

---

8. From Warfare to Welfare

The ultimate measure of governance is whether it serves life. Enlightened leadership and conscience-based institutions will redirect resources from warfare to welfare.

- Budgets once spent on bombs will fund schools and hospitals.

- Energy once poured into rivalry will fuel cooperation.

- Time once wasted on conflict will be devoted to creation.

This is not utopian. It is the practical result of recovery: freeing energy trapped in addiction and redirecting it to flourishing.

---

9. Call to Action

- **For Diplomats**: Frame governance reforms as recovery steps. Use the language of healing, not rivalry.

- **For Leaders**: Admit vulnerability. Walk the 12 steps personally and nationally. Model recovery.

- **For Citizens**: Support leaders who practice humility and conscience. Resist those addicted to power.

- **For Institutions**: Embed conscience audits and recovery practices. Create cultures of honesty, not denial.

- **For Movements**: Teach the 12 steps of peace. Train citizens in governance as recovery.

Conclusion: The Promise Fulfilled

The UN was founded to save humanity from war. That promise has been deferred but not destroyed. The path forward is clear: governance of humanity, by humanity, for humanity, with humanity.

This means institutions rooted in conscience. Leaders guided by witness. Citizens practicing recovery. A culture that admits shame, crosses the Fear Gap, and ends the need for war.

The 12-step pathway is not only for addicts in recovery rooms. It is for all of us, as a species. For we are all addicted to power, rivalry, and fear. And we can all recover, together.

PATH to Peace - A Preventative Armistice Treaty for Humanity

If we choose this path, we will fulfil the Charter's first words. We will save succeeding generations. We will prove that humanity can govern itself wisely.

This is the promise. This is the path. This is our future — if we dare to walk it.

Chapter 15. Turn to Humanity

Introduction: The Turning Point

Every journey has a moment when continuation on the old road is no longer possible. For humanity, that moment is now. Climate collapse, nuclear risk, mass displacement, technological disruption — all converge to show us that the old ways of governing are exhausted.

We cannot fight our way to safety. We cannot arm our way to trust. We cannot bomb our way to security. The only way forward is to **turn**: to turn from fear to conscience, from sovereignty to stewardship, from warfare to welfare.

This is not rhetoric. It is survival. The turn to humanity is the most urgent decision of our time.

1. The Limitation of "Defence of the Realm"

The UK, as one of the P5, has long articulated the doctrine that *"The first purpose of government is the defence of the realm."*

On one level, this statement is true. Government exists to protect people from harm. Defence is a core responsibility. But the doctrine is limited in two ways:

1. **Narrowness of "the realm"**: It assumes the realm is bounded by borders, defined by sovereignty, defended against outsiders. In an interconnected world, this definition is obsolete. Viruses, carbon, and nuclear fallout do not respect borders. Defence of one nation cannot be separated from defence of all.

2. **Militarisation of "defence"**: The doctrine assumes defence means weapons, armies, deterrence. But in reality, weapons now create as much insecurity as they prevent. Nuclear arsenals invite annihilation. Military budgets divert resources from welfare. Defence, in its old meaning, has become a danger.

Clinging to this outdated doctrine, the UK and its fellow P5 nations perpetuate the very risks they claim to counter. The "defence of the realm" has become the addiction of the realm.

---

2. The Potential of "Defence of the Realm"

Yet the doctrine also carries hidden potential — if we expand its meaning.

What if "the realm" were redefined as the whole human realm — the one planet, one atmosphere, one body of humanity we all share?

- To defend the realm would mean to defend humanity itself.

- Defence would mean preventing nuclear war, not threatening it.

- Defence would mean protecting ecosystems, not exploiting them.

- Defence would mean ensuring welfare, not waging warfare.

In this expanded sense, the doctrine could become a rallying cry for conscience: *the first purpose of government is the defence of humanity and the planet.*

Here lies the pivot. From limitation to potential. From narrow sovereignty to shared stewardship. From the UK's old doctrine to a universal one.

---

3. The PATH to Peace

This is why the Preventative Armistice Treaty of Humanity (PATH) matters. It operationalises this expanded defence:

- **No first use of nuclear weapons.**

- **Phased disarmament under verification.**

- **Confidential risk reporting, modelled on aviation safety.**

- **Empowered UNGA, with a Conscience Council.**

- **UN Parliamentary Assembly, giving humanity a voice.**

The PATH is not utopian. It is the treaty we will sign after World War III if we fail to act. The choice is simply whether we sign it now, in foresight, or later, in regret.

---

4. The Final Step of Recovery

In Chapter 12, we outlined a 12-step pathway out of humanity's addiction to war. The final step is to **carry the message**. Recovery is not private; it is shared. Those who awaken must guide others. Those who heal must serve the whole.

This is what the Turn to Humanity means. It is the carrying of the message — to citizens, leaders, institutions, and generations to come. It is the declaration that humanity has turned, that the addiction is broken, that conscience is now our compass.

---

5. The Voice of "We the Peoples"

The United Nations began with the words: *"We the Peoples."* Those words are not a preamble to be ignored; they are a mandate to be fulfilled. They declare that the highest authority is not the P5, not the Security Council, not even states themselves — but the peoples of the world united in conscience.

The Turn to Humanity is the fulfilment of that promise. It is the moment when "We the Peoples" rise to claim our authority, to declare that we are the real superpower, to insist that governance be by humanity, for humanity, with humanity.

---

6. Call to Action

- **For Leaders**: Redefine defence. Your realm is humanity. Your weapons are conscience. Your duty is stewardship.

- **For Diplomats**: Champion the PATH in the General Assembly. Use Article 22 to create the UNPA. Elevate conscience as authority.

- **For Citizens**: Carry the message. Speak of the end of war as possible. Demand leaders who serve humanity.

- **For Movements and Influencers**: Create narratives that show the turn — from warfare to welfare, from fear to conscience.

- **For the UNGA**: Stand tall. Break free of groupthink. Take the TPNW to the next level. Establish the PATH to Peace before catastrophe.

Conclusion: The Turn Has Come

Humanity is at a fork in the road. One path leads to catastrophe, the other to transformation. One is paved with fear, shame, and weapons. The other with conscience, stewardship, and shared humanity.

The doctrine of "defence of the realm" reveals both the danger and the promise. In its narrow sense, it keeps us addicted to war. In its expanded sense, it becomes the watchword of survival: the defence of humanity itself.

PATH to Peace - A Preventative Armistice Treaty for Humanity

The time has come to choose. To turn. To fulfil the Charter's first words. To declare that we no longer need war. To govern ourselves with conscience. To defend not just borders, but the human realm.

This is the campaign. This is the call.

Turn to Humanity — Follow the PATH to Peace — From Warfare to Welfare.

With Governance of Humanity, for Humanity, By Humanity, with Humanity.

Lincoln's words for a nation now extend to the planet. This book sets out the architecture of transformed global governance: the UNGA as the chamber of humanity, the UN Parliamentary Assembly as a people's voice, and the Conscience Council as the higher standard of truth and legitimacy. It dismantles the outdated Security Council paradigm and sketches a future where governance is not about domination, but about stewardship of humanity and Earth.

Turn to Humanity:

The final chapter gathers the threads into a unifying call: Turn to Humanity — follow the PATH to Peace — from Warfare to Welfare. It is both a credo and an invitation. Here, the principles are distilled into a simple declaration: that humanity is the real superpower, that conscience is our highest authority, and that by changing our perspective we change our future. It closes as both a summary of principles and a rallying cry for action.

Closing Declaration

Closing Declaration

The United Nations was founded to save succeeding generations from war. "The UN was not created to take mankind to heaven, but to save humanity from hell," was famously said by Dag Hammarskjöld. Now the UN needs to, at least, aim for Heaven or we will all go to nuclear Hell.

The PATH to Peace is before us. The ladders of transformation stand ready. The institutions of conscience can be built. The addiction to war can be healed. There is only one way out of the hell of addiction: upwards!

The legal treaty process for this change must begin within the First Committee of the United Nations. That was where the Nobel-Peace-Prize-Winning ICAN movement (The International Campaign Against Nuclear Weapons) started to become the Treaty on the Prohibition of Nuclear Weapons. This is the urgently necessary follow-on treaty, with working code-name ICAN-2, applicable to each diplomat, leader and person on the planet, representing perhaps:

The International Campaign for Accountable Nations.

What remains is the choice. To see the next paradigm shift in perspective. To govern not by fear, not by rivalry, not by shame — but by humanity. Let's at least aim to build Heaven on Earth, rather than continue to follow the current path to Hell … Press the Reboot button - quickly!

PATH to Peace - A Preventative Armistice Treaty for Humanity

Turn to Humanity:

—Follow the PATH to Peace

— From Warfare to Welfare.

With the Governance of Humanity, for Humanity, by Humanity,

And ... *with Humanity*, **rather than inhumanity.**

We the Peoples of the Future

We remember the years of fear,
 when nations bristled with weapons,
 and leaders mistook power for safety,
 and sovereignty for salvation.

We remember the shadows of mistrust,
 treaties signed in trembling,
 the silence of the bullied,
 the arrogance of the bullies.

And then — the turning.
 Not in war,
 not in ashes,
 but in conscience.

The halls of the United Nations
 filled with voices that would not yield,
 a chorus rising —
 We the Peoples.

No longer petitioners to the powerful,
 but the power itself.
 No longer scattered voices,
 but a parliament of humanity,
 a council of conscience.

PATH to Peace - A Preventative Armistice Treaty for Humanity

From warfare to welfare,
 from addiction to recovery,
 from fear to faith,
 we built anew.

The UN was not abolished —
 it was reborn.
 Its walls became transparent,
 its words became deeds,
 its treaties became trust.

Now we govern together,
 not by the veto of the few,
 but by the voice of all.
 Governance of Humanity,
 for Humanity,
 by Humanity,
 with Humanity.

We look back with gratitude —
 for those who turned first,
 for those who dared to trust,
 for those who held the path open
 until all could walk it.

And we know this truth:
 Peace is not the silence after war.
 Peace is the music of trust,
 played by all peoples,
 in one rhythm,
 for one world.

Anthem of the Peoples

We the Peoples, we arose,
 from the ruins, from the woes.
 No more bullies, no more war,
 Conscience opened every door.

From the ashes, trust was born,
 Night gave way to brighter dawn.
 UN's halls became our voice,
 Humanity became our choice.

Governance of all, we say,
 For Humanity, here to stay.
 By Humanity, justice true,
 With Humanity, we renew.

Turned to peace, our path made clear,
 Faith replaced the reign of fear.
 We the Peoples, joined as one,
 Earth's new age has now begun.

Chant of the Peoples

We the Peoples — one, not few!
 For Humanity — just and true!
 By Humanity — trust restored!
 With Humanity — peace assured!

400-Word Summary

The PATH to Peace argues that humanity stands at a turning point: either stumble into nuclear World War III or deliberately choose a preventative peace. The book begins by exposing the collapse of the sovereignty system born at Westphalia. National "defence of the realm" is obsolete in an interdependent world where WMDs, climate collapse, and systemic risks cross all borders. The P5/N9 are revealed as "WMD Villains," trapped in fear of humiliation, escalating weapons to mask shame. Yet villains can become heroes — by shifting their attention from fear to humanity's shared survival.

The book sets out the tools of transformation: the **Fear Gap** (why fear creates what it resists), the **Ladders** (truth, conscience, vitality), and **witness consciousness** (the inner stance that disarms projection). It then grounds these in institutions: a **Conscience Council** to hold leaders to moral standards, and a **UN Parliamentary Assembly** to give humanity itself a voice.

Law-making is examined as the anchor of trust: **objective harm belongs to law, subjective offence belongs to dialogue, predictability builds legitimacy**. Shame is revealed as the hidden driver of conflict — and its admission as the gateway to reconciliation.

The central proposal follows: a **Preventative Armistice Treaty of Humanity (PATH)**, to be signed before catastrophe. Every war ends with a treaty; the point is to sign one in foresight, not regret. This requires recognising that war is not a necessity but an addiction — and adopting a 12-step recovery pathway for leaders and nations.

PATH to Peace - A Preventative Armistice Treaty for Humanity

Objections about enforcement are answered: not with more weapons, but with **legitimacy, verification, incentives, precedent, education, and recovery culture**. Historical examples — the Cuban Missile Crisis, the Berlin Wall, Ireland, South Africa — prove peaceful enforcement works when bullies are not shielded by bigger bullies.

The book closes with a call for **enlightened leadership**: integrated, shame-aware, conscience-guided. It culminates in a redefinition of defence itself: not defence of borders, but defence of humanity and the planet.

The campaign line is clear:

Turn to Humanity — Follow the PATH to Peace — From Warfare to Welfare.

With Governance of Humanity, for Humanity, by Humanity, with Humanity.

100-Word Summary

The PATH to Peace shows how humanity can prevent World War III by signing a **Preventative Armistice Treaty** before catastrophe. It unmasks the P5/N9 as "WMD Villains" trapped in fear, and offers transformation through conscience, witness, and shame-awareness. Institutions like a **Conscience Council** and **UN Parliamentary Assembly** can anchor legitimacy, while law must focus on objective harm, leaving offence to dialogue. Enforcement comes through legitimacy, verification, incentives, precedent, and education, not weapons. War is reframed as addiction — and recovery as leadership. The call is simple:

Turn to Humanity - Follow the PATH to Peace - From Warfare to Welfare

With Governance of Humanity, for Humanity, by Humanity, with Humanity.

The preamble to the UNESCO Constitution states:

"Since wars begin in the minds of men, it is in the minds of men that the defenses of peace must be constructed"

"When we choose dialogue over violence, we tap into the immense potential for transformative change, realizing that conflict is not an end in itself, but an opportunity for growth and reconciliation" [ChatGPT]

About the Author

Gordon (Gordan[(R)]) Glass is a transformational supercoach serving discreetly at Board levels in businesses, governments and NGO/CSOs. He has over 50 years experience of UN topics and intergovernmental meetings, especially in nuclear weapons, and over 35 years' training and practice with intimate personal, organisational and institutional coaching skills.

He focuses on developing global leadership to transform global governance, and has spent his lifetime participating in many varied, large scale, long term, transformational societal projects, including in the UK and law, developing an extraordinary inter-disciplinary range of unusual skills and techniques.

Gordon works through his company, Global Leadership Ltd with the trading name of Government Dynamics® at

PATH to Peace - A Preventative Armistice Treaty for Humanity www.government-dynamics.com, to build trust and flow in global governance and politics: Going beyond conflict: Now as a TruthFinder.

Other books by Gordan Glass® on Amazon

Series 1: Global Leadership 101: (2014-15)

1. The President's Legacy: The world is waiting ...

2. The Nuclear War Game: Transforming Global Security

3. Transforming Global Politics: To make it attractive, engaging, transparent, effective and trustworthy

4. Government Dynamics: Building Trust in Politics

5. Resolving Terrorism: Resolution Without Compromise

6. The Heathrow Report 2015: What the Airports Commission Missed

Series 2: **GPT-4 Speaks Out:** - (2023)

1. GPT-4 Speaks Out...: On UN Reform - to Avoid Nuclear War

2. GPT-4 Speaks Out...: On AI Global Risks, Public Policy & Itself

3. GPT-4 Speaks Out...: On Global Warming, Climate Change & Itself

4. GPT-4 Speaks Out...: On Financial Risks & UNGA Treaty Project

5. GPT-4 Speaks Out...: With Poems to End War

6. GPT-4 Speaks Out...: On Customer Service & UNGA Treaty Project

7. GPT-4 Speaks Out...: Leaders Take Heed!

PATH to Peace - A Preventative Armistice Treaty for Humanity

Series 3: **Abolishing Nuclear Weapons: (2023)**

1. Abolishing Nuclear Weapons: The Current State of Play

2. Abolishing Nuclear Weapons: Changing the Game

3. Abolishing Nuclear Weapons: The Way of Insight

4. Abolishing Nuclear Weapons: Future Global Governance

5. Abolishing Nuclear Weapons: UNGA - Ethical Leadership

6. Abolishing Nuclear Weapons: Global Peace, Freedom & Security

7. Abolishing Nuclear Weapons: Villains into Heroes

Series 4: **Using AI…: (2023/2024)**

1. Using AI to Regulate Human Behaviour - On Social Media Platforms

2. Using AI to Transform Global Governance

3. Using AI to Transform the United Nations: Through the UNGA Pact for the Future

4. Using AI to Transform the Nuclear Weapons Divide

5. AI on Overconfident Leadership: Hubris & Nemesis

6. Using AI to EstablishGlobal Principles: to End War

7. AI-Peacemaker.com: To Transform Conflicts

Series 5: Why World War III? (2024)

1. Why World War III? Global Warming or Nuclear Winter?

2. Abuses of Power at the UN - With Essential Actions

3. The Major Powers at War: Now Escalation Rules

Series 6: Going Beyond Conflicts ... (2024/5)

1. Highway Robbery: The Banes of Road Closures

2. Beyond Shame: Lies the Promised Land

Series 7: The White Smoke of Divine Guidance (2025)

(Produced in the Papal Succession Period - April/May)

1. *LAUNCH*: Starting & Stopping WWIII

2. Transforming Revelations: A New Perspective for Humanity

3. Villains to Heroes: Humanising Global Leadership

4. Healing the World: The Next Step for Humanity

5. The Truth of Peace & Love: For the Evolution of Humanity

6. World Peace By Insight: War Becomes Unthinkable

7. Middle East Peace: The End of the Enemy

8. The Search for Truth and Trust: Our Future is in Conscience

Series 8: The Birth of a Global Movement

1. The Broken Ladder of Truth: How to Fix it for Good

2. AI Truth Leadership Index:
      And Strategic Defence Review

3. Saving Humanity:
      Evolution's Next Step

4. Competence & Conscience Indexes:
      …

5. Turn to Humanity - Book 1:
      Lawlessness & Inhumanity

6. Turn to Humanity - Book 2:
      Crossing the Fear Gap

7. Turn to Humanity - Book 3:
      Rebirth into Wholeness

8. PATH to Peace - Book 4:
      A Preventative Armistice Treaty for Humanity

**To order: Follow the QR code overleaf
To Gordan Glass at Amazon.com
via** bit.ly/3VcLsPw